T0147314

Leaning Into The Light

Sheila S. Dembowski

iUniverse, Inc.
Bloomington

iUniverse books may be ordered through booksellers or by contacting:

iUniverse
1663 Liberty Drive
Bloomington, IN 47403
www.iuniverse.com
1-800-Authors (1-800-288-4677)

ISBN: 978-1-4502-9733-2 (sc)
ISBN: 978-1-4502-9734-9 (ebook)

Printed in the United States of America

iUniverse rev. date: 02/18/2011

I dedicate this book:

To my family, especially my parents, Margaret and Patrick Connors, for always being there for me.

Love conquers all things; let us surrender to love.

—Virgil

To my husband, Jim, and our son, Michael, whose love and patience are never taken for granted.

Sometimes being cured is found in the touch of someone you love.

—Michael J. Fox

To all of my friends, especially Lois Rakowski, who showed me how a person can look death in the eye and still have a positive grace that inspires.

You are my lamp O Lord; the Lord turns my darkness into light.

—II Samuel 22:29

To all of the special teachers in my life, especially Sister Agnes Steiner, who taught me the importance of faith and service, and Sue Alberti, my high school English teacher, who gave me the confidence to become a teacher and a writer.

Flatter me and I may not believe you.
Criticize me and I may not like you.
Ignore me and I may not forgive you.
Encourage me and I will not forget you.

—*William Arthur Ward*

Finally, I want to express my gratitude to all the nurses, support staff and doctors I have encountered on this journey. I have been taken care of by many wonderful, dedicated individuals and I am truly grateful for them and all they do for others.

With God all things are possible.

—*Matthew 19:26*

Contents

Preface

To begin anew, we must say good-bye to who we once were.

—Anonymous

I started out writing this book for one person, our son, Michael. Looking back on it, the process of writing a memoir seemed more like an egotistical act—a written document that would immortalize my thoughts. But I wanted our son to know more about me and how my past shaped me into the person I am today. Hopefully this collection of essays will do just that.

However, for me, this book serves three additional purposes that can be summed up in three words: empathy, support, and explanation. I want to provide a clear account of my own personal experiences with chronic illness so that those who read it and have absolutely nothing to compare it to in their own lives can come away from this book with a better overall understanding of what a life with chronic health issues is all about.

Empathy is the key word, not sympathy. Most people with chronic illness who are dealing with it in a positive manner do not want others to feel sorry for them or their situations.

For those who may be going through the same issues I have, it is my hope that this book gives you another resource to turn to that inspires you on your own road to acceptance and gratitude.

And for those of you who know or love someone with chronic pain or health problems, I hope this book reminds you that unconditional love and patience are wonderful gifts to share with others, and they are among the greatest that can be given.

Chapter One

The Absence of Erica

Farming looks mighty easy when your plow is a pencil,
and you're a thousand miles from the cornfield.

—Dwight D. Eisenhower

A lock of brown hair, securely matted onto the railing of the stanchion. It was the last piece left of a part of my past. I stared at it for a while. The lights around me had begun to dim. I looked up. My sister was turning out the barn lights.

"It's time to go in," she said.

"All right," I replied.

As I started out the door, I turned back to reflect on what had happened.

They were all gone—all of them. The bright heifers, the spunky calves, the milking cows, old and young alike. They were all gone.

The barn was cold and empty. It was like standing in a tomb.

Barns should never be empty, I thought.

I closed the door and started walking toward the house. The mud was oozing beneath my boots. The tire tracks left by the cattle trucks had made deep ruts in the muddy driveway.

As I opened the door to the house, I could hear voices in the kitchen. I walked into the brightly lit room and saw my mother sitting at the table, surrounded by my brothers and sisters.

"It was for the best … we did the right thing, you'll see … don't worry, everything will be all right …"

My mother nodded slowly.

"Where's Dad?" I asked.

"He's in his new chair," my sister replied. "He's … feeling weak."

I entered the living room quietly and looked over toward him. His eyes were shut, but the pain was evident on his face. He seemed relaxed but looked pale and weak. We had bought him a new chair as a "welcome home from the hospital" gift. His heart attack had left him disabled and unable to work our family farm.

As I sat down next to him, I reached for his hand—worn from many years of hard labor—and squeezed it. His eyes opened.

"Hi, Fatso," he whispered.

"I'm glad you're back home," I replied.

Deciding to let him rest, I left his side and went into my bedroom.

I sat on my bed and stared out the window. Usually, the cows could be easily seen from where I was sitting. But now, all I saw was an empty barnyard.

I wonder how they will like their new home. I hope that no one will pick on Erica, I thought.

Erica was my pet. She was my favorite cow, and being one of only two red Holsteins made her even more unique.

I guess the reason I loved Erica so much was because I thought she liked me. The other members of the herd always picked on her. But if she ran to me, she was guaranteed protection.

I remember warm summer evenings when I would walk out to the pasture to move the cows toward the barn. The mild, gentle breezes of early evening would brush my face as I casually strode through the meadow.

By midsummer, the pasture had been neatly trimmed by the herd, except for small patches of tall, coarse grass scattered randomly. Among the bogs, the narrow, twisting cow path wound endlessly in different directions. An imaginary straight line could be drawn between the barnyard and the edge of the grassland, but cows, being the mysterious creatures they are, insisted on walking their own creative paths.

As I would approach the knolls at the back of the field, a killdeer might hop ahead of me, maintaining a certain nonchalance but always keeping a safe distance.

Then the cows would see me and begin their walk toward the barn. The older cows would rise slowly, like senior citizens out of their easy chairs, while the younger cows would jump up quickly and move hurriedly on their way.

And always, as she did every day, Erica would be the last to leave the pasture.

With her constantly by my side, we would walk back together. Whenever another cow would start taunting Erica, she would move closer, walking directly behind me and sometimes even stepping on the back of my heels. It was a little too close. In fact, it frightened me at times. If I would start to walk faster, Erica would keep pace right behind me, step for step all the way.

As we approached the barn, I would leave Erica outside to eat from the feeder wagon. This was the only time Erica was able to eat in comfort, because usually the other cows wouldn't allow her near the wagon.

After about an hour, Erica would approach the barn door and rub her head against it. This was her signal to let us know that she was through eating. I would open the door, and she would quickly trot in and find her usual place.

Although odd, this was her daily routine, and she followed it precisely.

Now, over twenty years later, I occasionally drive by our old farm. Many of the farms that thrived during my childhood now stand abandoned. A way of life that was once common is now slowly becoming extinct.

Our farm looks the same in many ways, but the pasture is no longer manicured. The grassy weeds grow tall and, if you look closely, you can still see faint hints of the crooked path that the cows traced on their trips to the barn. But this too will soon be erased, losing its battle with the encroaching grasses.

In my mind there also rages a battle—to retain the memories of Erica and her friends. A busy world is a demanding place, and the simple things in life are sometimes too easily forgotten.

But I am afraid I will lose the struggle. The absence of Erica, the desperate look of the pasture, the abandoned barns are but symbols of a lost past and an uncertain future. Life will go on, plans will be made, but a way of life has disappeared, and it can never be reclaimed.

Chapter Two

Mentors

The difference between stumbling blocks and stepping stones is the way one uses them.

—Anonymous

If a person looks back at her life and searches for those moments that made a difference, that may have reversed her destiny, sometimes she can discover more about herself and perhaps find the answer to the question, "What made me who I am today?"

At the time those events occurred, they might have seemed insignificant. But looking back, I am thankful for the experiences and, more importantly, the people who helped me get this far.

During my childhood, I had a wonderful teacher who also happened to be the principal of my elementary school, Sister Agnes. She taught me, through example, the importance of service and dedicating your life to helping others, especially those in need.

I remember one time in particular, when I was in sixth grade and we had a long-term substitute teacher filling in for our regular classroom teacher who was on maternity leave. My classmates were giving this teacher a very rough time, and at times, the class was completely out of control. Whenever Sister walked into the room, however, that stopped immediately. She was respected by even the most naughty of children.

One day, she called me down to her office, and we had a discussion about the classroom. She was asking me what was going on and if I had any suggestions as to how the situation could be changed. I was amazed at how she valued my comments, and I have never forgotten the feeling I had during that discussion. Children want to be valued. Even today, I use that lesson from so many years ago. As a teacher myself, I am always going out of my way to let students know that I appreciate their opinions.

The other teacher in my life who helped shape my future was one of my high school English teachers, Sue Alberti. My high school career was far from stellar, and my grades reflected that. Mrs. Alberti saw my writing talents in her composition class and encouraged me to write as much as I could, as often as I could. She submitted one of my stories to a writing competition at a nearby university. As a result, I got to go to a workshop at the campus and meet an actual author, who critiqued my work.

Mrs. Alberti also encouraged me to become a teacher, getting me to join the forensics team and work on my public-speaking skills. It was one of the scariest things I had ever done, but I did it despite my fears. I won first place in the Voice of Democracy contest and had to speak in front of a group of about sixty people. I practiced for two weeks, every day, until I had that speech memorized. I remember my father telling me to scan the audience and look over their heads at the back wall, so it would give the appearance that I was looking directly at them. That piece of advice must have worked, because I can still picture my teacher coming up to me after the speech with a beaming smile on her face.

When you are the target of bullying by your peers, as I was for most of my high school career, you need people beyond your parents to help you gain the confidence you are so desperately seeking. Mrs. Alberti and Sister Agnes made a huge difference in my life.

As a teacher myself, I know that our words and, more importantly, our actions speak volumes. Just a few years ago, I received a letter in the mail from a former student, now in high school, who was going to attend college to become a librarian. Her touching letter recalled how I had inspired her and how she wanted to do the same for others.

A man named Charles H. Spurgeon once said, "A good character is the best tombstone. Those who loved you and were helped by you will remember you when forget-me-nots have withered. Carve your name on hearts, not on marble."

If all of us lived our lives that way, wouldn't the world be a better place?

Chapter Three

Childhood Courage

Never look down on anybody unless you are helping them up.

—*Jesse Jackson*

Earlier I mentioned the people who made a positive difference in my life. Unfortunately, in everyone's life there are also situations—and people within those situations—who pull us in a negative direction. Their actions can be just as powerful, or sometimes even more so, than the positive influences.

My childhood was a happy one. I attended a very small parochial elementary school, my parents drove me to school and picked me up every day, and there were twelve students in my grade. That small-school atmosphere helped me blossom academically and socially.

Growing up on a dairy farm, with my older siblings having moved out for the most part by the time I was about nine years old, I essentially lived the life of an only child. This had benefits and disadvantages.

The turning point in my childhood was the transition from sixth to seventh grade. In seventh grade, I started at a public school junior high that was much larger than my old school. The small, family-like atmosphere was replaced by a large, institutional one. The number of students in my grade went from twelve to two hundred. I no longer had a desk in which to store my supplies—now I had a locker, shared with a total stranger, with a padlock combination that created more than its share of awkward moments.

Most significantly, during that time I became the target of bullying by a group of girls, led by one in particular. The verbal harassment by a bunch of female thugs would make the two years of junior high the most disturbing portion of my life.

Bullying comes in many forms, and so did mine. It would begin in the morning at 6:50 AM when I walked onto the school bus. Finding an empty seat was so important. If for some reason the bus was filled, and you had to share a seat, you were setting yourself up for a possible unpleasant verbal exchange. Early on during that first year, I innocently sat down next to a girl when there were other open seats on the bus. I was new and shy and was just trying to make new friends. This girl turned and looked at me with an expression of total disgust. "What the hell do you think you're doing?" she growled. "Get off my seat, you ugly bitch."

I was shocked by both her statement and by the fact that she was so incredibly young to have become such a foul-mouthed, bitter individual. Unfortunately, I would encounter many more of those comments in the future, and the type of people who make them.

When you are the target of a bully, your self-esteem is basically crushed. It takes many years of therapy, both self-help and professional, to guide you back in the right direction.

When people whose only goal is to make you so miserable you will cry in public surround you on a daily basis, life can become more than just uncomfortable. It can affect your destiny in a negative way. It can make you withdraw from the person God meant for you to be.

Instead of looking at all of your good qualities, negative people seem to get great joy out of watching you flounder and doubt yourself. The bully's own small self-esteem is built up purely on the basis of watching his or her victim's self-esteem slowly disappear. What a sad, sick process.

In high school, the taunts and ridicule seemed to let up somewhat. I had found my own little niche in the pathetically petty and meaningless high school social scene. Most days, I just went to school in survival mode, praying that the bullies were having a good day by leaving me alone and that I would have a good day by not encountering any of them, especially in a social situation where I was alone and surrounded by more than one of them.

When I was a junior in high school, my father had a massive heart attack, became disabled, and could no longer work. To help earn some extra money, I started working as a janitor's assistant after school, sweeping floors.

I hated the job, but I really needed the money, so as soon as the last bell rang, I literally ran to the cafeteria and started pulling chairs out from under the tables as fast as I could. I needed to get the first four sets done before "the crowd" came to hang out after school.

Most days I would make it, but once in a while if I got there late, they would already be sitting there, either on the tables themselves or in the chairs. Then I would be forced to walk up to them and ask them to move. Sometimes people would smile and get up and walk away in a civil fashion. But most of the time, there would be those few who felt great joy in throwing garbage on the floor, watching me pick it up, and then slamming their chairs—all the while calling me mean, sometimes even vulgar names.

That was a negative experience that taught me something very valuable. Every person doing a job deserves respect, regardless of their appearance, social status, or educational background.

As I write this, I can still feel my anger, feel the outsides of my ears burning, feel the pent-up rage for something that happened over twenty-five years ago.

I was determined from that point forward that—dumb, ugly, poor, whatever the label I was given—I was not going to be defined by bullies. My life had meaning and purpose. I was going to move forward from this.

I applied to go to college.

Chapter Four

Good-bye, Grandpa

Blessed are they that mourn; for they shall be comforted.

—Matthew 5:4

As I entered the church, I saw him lying there surrounded by bouquets of flowers. I turned around for a brief moment. My father and mother, uncle and aunt were close behind. My cousins and my brother and sister were following them. I turned and continued to walk toward the casket. When I reached the front of the church, I looked at him. He was wearing a dark suit and had a peaceful expression on his face. Everyone gathered around the casket, and we took turns praying.

Little by little, more relatives and friends came and expressed the words that are customarily exchanged at times like this—words that both mean so much yet say so little.

As the evening continued and more people arrived, the atmosphere changed. People began to talk about the old days. Some laughed and some cried.

As I sat there looking at him, my eyes drifted to his hands. I remembered a game we used to play together when I was a little girl. It had no particular name, but I suppose if it were given one, it would be called cats and dogs. We would place our hands on a table. I would pretend to be a cat and use my fingers as a cat would use its legs. He would do the same, except he was the dog. Then we would pretend to fight one another. The cat would usually win, even though it was much smaller and not as wise as the dog.

9

A hand on my shoulder startled me. It was my sister.

"We'll have to go soon," she whispered.

The crowd began to slowly disperse, and it became time to say our last good-bye. The family took turns kneeling and praying around the coffin. Finally, after the church was nearly empty, I was left there with my sister. We kneeled and began to pray. My eyes filled with tears, and I found I could not hold them back. As I softly sobbed, my sister whispered to him, "We love you. We love you." I reached out and lightly touched his hand. It felt cold.

"No," she said, "touch his sleeve. It will feel more natural."

She gently lifted my hand and placed it on his sleeve. She was right.

"Good-bye," I whispered. I stood up, turned away, and walked quickly down the aisle.

When I arrived at his house, many relatives were already there. I went into the dining room where everyone was gathered around the table, discussing memories. I listened for about an hour. Then I quietly excused myself and left the room.

I drifted slowly up the staircase, gazing at the portraits that hung along the wall. One was a painting of my grandmother when she was about my age. It was beautiful. By the time I reached the room I always thought of as mine, I was completely exhausted. I slowly undressed and went directly to bed.

From below, I could hear the constant buzz of conversation, the laughter of children. That's what this house was always about—laughter, security, and the joy of family. That night did not appear to be any different from the nights that had come before it. But it was.

As I lay there, I remembered that last time I had seen him. It was a hot, sunny day and we had taken him to visit the farm where he was born. All that remained were the foundations, and even they had become overwhelmed with weeds. Even though there weren't any buildings standing, he didn't seem to mind.

We were busy peppering him with questions. What had the house looked like? How many cows? Horses? He seemed more than willing to answer, but as I look back now, I can see that perhaps his mind recalled many things not related to the questions he answered.

Instead, in his mind's eye, he saw not the weed-covered, barren valley we saw, but the busy, bustling turn-of-the-century farm of his youth. And the voices he heard were not those of today's inquisitive relatives but of his father and mother, brothers and sister as they bantered back and forth while performing their routine tasks on this beautiful farm in this beautiful valley. And the world, for just one brief moment, was the world that gave joy to his youth.

He enjoyed seeing his old farm, and by the end of the day, we were all glad we had taken him there. When the day came to an end and we had to say good-bye, I remember thinking how old he was getting and how happy I was that he had gotten to see his old farm.

I will always remember seeing him on the porch at the end of that day, waving as we drove away.

These good memories allowed me to sleep, and the long night passed.

We buried him the next morning. That which we could see was gone, but what he was, who he was, is mine to keep in my heart forever.

As we drove away from his house for the last time, I looked back, and the familiar porch was empty. But my heart—my heart was full.

Good-bye, Grandpa.

Chapter Five

Commencement

Go confidently in the direction of your dreams.
Live the life you have imagined.

—Henry David Thoreau

To an outsider, the dorm room might appear to be cluttered and cramped. But to me, it was home. A temporary home, at least.

On my bookshelf, books were piled to the ceiling; papers were scattered over the desk. The large chip on the right side of the desk was still there, as it had been for the last three years and would probably remain for another twenty. The school was not very efficient when it came to making small repairs.

The other desk was covered with boxes, some containing small appliances like my hot plate, toaster oven, and can opener. One box was solely dedicated to a variety of pans I had collected from the Salvation Army. My favorite appliance was the miniature electric frying pan. I had only paid three dollars for it, and it had definitely paid for itself several hundred times over. In later years, I've fondly remembered the greasy toasted-cheese sandwiches and fried eggs I lived off of so easily during those college days.

I slowly packed those items that brought back vivid memories of people and places that had touched my life. I grasped and hugged the two blue-and-yellow pillows tightly and took a deep breath. They faintly smelled of the candles that were in my parents' house, where my mother so lovingly sewed them for me. Whenever things got difficult, I had found comfort in those small pillows. Touching them seemed to bring my mother a little bit closer.

As I placed the pillows in a plastic bag, the doll caught the corner of my eye. Jeanne had brought it back from her trip to Russia. I couldn't remember what Jeanne had called it, but I remembered seeing a doll like it on *Sesame Street* as a child. It was one of those dolls that can be taken apart in the middle, and each time, a smaller doll can be found inside. I loved the bright hand-painted colors. I picked the doll up and looked at the bottom of it. I had kept the original price tag, written in Russian. Special friends like Jeanne would be missed most of all.

I had already taken down the dozens of posters that lined the walls and the bulletin boards. Michael J. Fox was my favorite and had been since high school. His image was inescapable—Michael standing, Michael sitting, Michael leaning against a tree... Just months earlier, they hadn't seemed as childish as they did now. It was funny how even within a year I had changed so much.

In my hurry, I had almost forgotten to open the cupboard next to my bed. There I had several cans of assorted vegetables and boxes filled with macaroni and cheese. Three coffee mugs and some plastic silverware lined one side. In the corner, I found what appeared to be the remains of a dehydrated apple. I suddenly remembered that several months earlier, one of my third-graders had given it to me. His name was Bobby, and I recalled his bright smile and freckled face.

As the boxes piled up, the room began to take on the appearance it usually had during the beginning of the fall season. Stark, bare, lemon-colored walls contrasted with the navy-blue curtains, which probably hadn't been properly cleaned since Nixon was president.

Two beds lined the walls. I used one as a couch and the other as my official bed. Looking back, I wonder how people could live so closely together in harmony. However, at the time I first moved in as a junior, this room seemed more than adequate. It served its purpose. It was warm and cozy. It was sufficient, and soon it would become only a memory.

Then I remembered that I needed to move the dresser back from inside the closet to its original spot. As I began to drag the dresser across the floor, I looked down and saw a small hole in the wall, just about three inches from the floor. I bent over and examined it more closely.

The hole brought to mind a story I had heard my father tell many times before. For several years, my family vacationed at a resort in northern

Wisconsin. The cabin my parents rented had a small hole in the wall, and my dad would leave a handwritten note every year. It said simply, "See you again next year."

I suddenly began to think about all of those students who had lived in my room before me. Who were they, and what had become of them? Did they have the same dreams I had?

A knock came at the door. It was my parents, asking me if I was ready to start packing the car. As my parents each left with boxes, I walked over to my desk and picked up my journal. Opening it to the back page, I tore out the copy of the poem I had submitted to the graduation committee. It was to be printed in the graduation program, but I felt like reading it again.

A Moment in Time
By Sheila Connors, Class of '92

Commence
  1. *to enter upon: see begin*

Music begins. All in rows.
March. Sit. Listen. Daydream.
My name.
I walk to the stage.
One foot in
Front of the
Other.
Covered with the badges of
Intellect.
Firmly shake hands.
"Congratulations."
"Thank you."
Smile, come on, smile.
I walk off the stage. Every step
Represents each semester, every test,
Every paper, every lecture …
One foot in
Front of the
Other.
Face the crowd.

I smile and nod at strangers I
Will never see again.
Tears fill my eyes. One escapes
Down my cheek.
"Is this the end or ..."

Commence
    1. *to enter upon: see begin.*

    I walked back over to the closet and bent over, gingerly pushing the poem into the crevice. Then I went back to work packing.

Chapter Six

The Beginning

It is during our darkest moments that we must focus to see the light.

—*Taylor Benson*

On my thirtieth birthday, I found myself in a position that I, quite frankly, had never thought I would be in. I was engaged, and I was incredibly happy.

For several years, I'd had a great job, and suddenly I had found my soul mate—someone I truly felt I was meant to be with for the rest of my life.

Then, six months after we were engaged, it happened.

One morning I woke up and there it was. I kept blinking, but it didn't stop for several minutes. Everywhere I looked, I had double vision. The first image I usually saw when I woke up was a giant Tigger stuffed animal sitting at the foot of my bed. Jim, my fiancé, had given it to me after I had mentioned how I had a Tigger when I was a child and always slept with it.

After the double vision subsided, I went on with my schedule, which included a full day of teaching. I had been working as an elementary-school librarian for seven years, and although it was a stressful and demanding job at times, it was what I had been dedicating my life to and was a very enjoyable part of my life.

During the day, I was still having an occasional incident of blurry vision, and I mentioned to my assistant at the time what had happened that morning.

"I had a really bad migraine yesterday," I said. "Maybe that's affecting my eyesight."

"Can you look at me again?" she asked.

"Sure, why?" I questioned.

"Your right eyelid is drooping. Has it ever done that before?"

Strange, I thought. I went and looked in the mirror in the back room. Sure enough, it was.

I called at lunchtime and made an appointment with my eye doctor. By the time I met with him a few days later, the double vision had worsened.

He examined me and suggested I contact my family doctor. I got in to see her the next day, late in the afternoon. She was concerned immediately and ordered an MRI of my brain. Her first concern was a stroke or a tumor.

The MRI was a difficult experience, but looking back on it, what was to come would be nothing in comparison.

Lying in the coffin-like tube, listening to the screeches and the loud clicking sounds of the machine, I let my imagination run wild.

Do I have a tumor or did I have a stroke? How could this be happening to me?

I sat in an empty waiting room long after my doctor's office had closed. I kept staring at the huge aquarium, trying to settle my nerves. It had been a few hours since the test.

I heard a door open and a familiar voice say, "Come on back, Sheila. Let's talk."

My doctor sat me down and told me that there was nothing significant in the MRI, no evidence of a tumor. She made an appointment for me with an eye surgeon. My symptoms were troubling.

For the next few days, I tried to go on with my life as usual. My fiancé, Jim, was concerned yet upbeat. He assured me that it couldn't be too serious or the test results would have reflected that. We had high hopes that the eye surgeon would have some answers.

It turned out he did. But the answer was not what we wanted to hear.

Chapter Seven

The Medical Freak

My God, I have no idea where I am going. I do not see the road ahead of me. I cannot know for certain where it will end ... but I will not fear, for you are ever with me.

—*Thomas Merton*

I have never been a person who feels at ease in situations where I don't have complete control. Call it a Type A personality; call it whatever you like. I think that most people who find themselves in circumstances that don't have clear answers feel uncomfortable.

Sitting in the eye surgeon's exam room, I prayed that there would be some kind of answers to the many questions I had—most importantly, what was wrong with me and how could it be treated?

The technicians I dealt with were pleasant and appeared concerned. I answered many of the same questions again that I had been asked by both my own eye doctor and my general practitioner. Throughout the coming years, I would find myself repeating my medical history over and over again.

The eye surgeon came in and introduced himself. He scanned some papers and proceeded to examine me. Within minutes, he was testing my vision by covering one eye and observing the other's reaction.

"Amazing ..." he said to himself.

"What?" I asked.

Without answering my question, he suddenly left the room and returned a few moments later with what I think was another eye doctor. I'm not certain, because we were not introduced.

"Watch this," he told her. He repeated the procedure. While one eye was covered, the other eyelid opened extra wide. This overreaction was an important clue in my diagnosis.

He continued to move from one eye to the other. "This is something you only read about—it's so rare to actually see one of these in person."

The two of them continued to talk to one another as if I were not even in the room. It was a humiliating and helpless feeling. Unfortunately, it was the first of many I would experience over the years. When you have a rare illness, sometimes those in the medical field lose sight of who you are as a person and only see an opportunity to observe a medical rarity.

Another test followed. This one involved injecting a chemical into the bloodstream that tests muscle reaction. It lasted only a few minutes, but it seemed like an eternity as muscles throughout my entire face twitched, contracted, and convulsed uncontrollably. My eyelids were going up and down, my lips moved horizontally and vertically at the same time. I begged him to stop it.

"Relax," he said. "It will be over soon."

When all was said and done, he told me I had something called myasthenia gravis, and that I should see a neurologist for treatment. He would set up an appointment.

He left the room—and left me with even more questions than when I entered.

When he returned, I asked him to again tell me the name of this disease. He tore off a piece of paper and wrote it down.

"You can go on the Internet and look it up," he said. "Your appointment is in about a month. The neurologist can prescribe medication."

"But what do I do in the meantime?" I asked.

"What do you mean?"

"I have such bad double vision … I can't drive a car, I'm having a hard time at work …" I felt completely lost. Why couldn't this man see that?

He pulled open a drawer and handed me a plastic eye patch that fits over the lens on a pair of eyeglasses.

"Wear this. That should help somewhat."

I stared at him in disbelief.

"So you can't prescribe me any medication for this?" I felt like I was begging. "What am I supposed to do for the next month?"

He was already starting out the door. He turned and looked at me, almost irritated.

"Learn to live with it," he said coldly.

I have to admit that this was one of the darkest moments of my life. I walked out to the car, where Jim was waiting for me. Our next stop was home and an Internet search that would end up giving me more information and more inspiration than ever to find answers to my questions.

Chapter Eight

One Step

*Therefore encourage one another, and build up
one another, just as you also are doing.*

—I Thessalonians 5:11

Sitting at my computer, I tried to focus on the task that lay before me. Being a librarian and having my background and passion in research, I knew what I had to do in order to find out more about this mystery disease I was now supposed to have.

I double-checked my spelling and started my research journey, a journey that continues on and off to this day.

I discovered the Myasthenia Gravis Foundation website and read everything I could find. Their explanation of the disease gave me the background I needed. According to the website:

> Myasthenia Gravis comes from the Greek and Latin words meaning "grave muscular weakness." The most common form of MG is a chronic autoimmune neuromuscular disorder that is characterized by fluctuating weakness of the voluntary muscle groups …

Common symptoms can include:

- A drooping eyelid

- Blurred or double vision

- Slurred speech

- Difficulty chewing and swallowing

- Weakness in the arms and legs

- Chronic muscle fatigue

- Difficulty breathing

The list of symptoms was scary, especially since I was having more than just the double vision and drooping eyelid. I had noticed in the last few months at school how my voice was becoming weaker by the end of the day, and I would find the sensation of my throat closing in and the nasally tone of my voice disturbing. Now everything was making more sense as I started to put together the pieces of the puzzle.

My mind was racing. *What is going to happen to me? What is my next step?* Those who know me well will agree with me when I say I am an over-thinker. If I were to have played a role in the movie *Dances With Wolves*, my name would have been "Woman Who Thinks Too Much."

I did not want to become an invalid. I did not want to have someone taking care of me. At that moment, my future suddenly seemed quite bleak.

Then I realized there was a shadow on the screen. I looked over my shoulder and saw Jim standing there, reading what I was reading.

I turned to him and said, "You know ... if you want to forget about getting married, I would understand."

He looked at me with a puzzled expression.

"What are you talking about?" he said.

"Well ..." I stammered.

"Sheila, I love you very much, and nothing is going to change that. I have waited my whole life to meet someone like you, and God wouldn't bring us together if He didn't think we belonged together."

I got up from my chair and we embraced.

He held me tightly and whispered in my ear, "You will beat this ... I know you will. And I will be there for you, every step of the way."

It is said that the longest journeys begin the same as the shortest, with the first step. This was my first step—our first step—into the unknown. But at least we were together on the journey.

Chapter Nine

Fear Is Your Greatest Enemy

Miracles happen to those who believe in them.

—*Bernard Berenson*

I returned to my family doctor a few days later and told her about my experience with the eye surgeon. She was very upset about how he treated me, and she got me in to see a neurologist in two days instead of a month. I was very grateful.

When I went to the neurologist, he did more tests, including one where my muscles had electrical currents sent through them to measure their reaction. It was an excruciating experience, and I wouldn't wish it on my worst enemy.

He concluded that I did have MG, and we discussed my treatment options. I had done a lot of research and asked about surgery. He did not recommend it because of the risk involved. He thought medication would be best for now.

I am a person who questions everything, especially if I feel that I am right. I wasn't convinced that medication was the answer. I wanted a chance at remission.

"How will I know if the disease has gotten worse and spread to my arms?" I asked.

He was honest in his answer. "Well, if you go to comb your hair, and you can't lift the brush, then you will know it has spread."

I didn't like that answer, so I kept looking for different ones.

My sister called me a few days later and told me about a friend of hers who also had MG. This woman was seeing a neurologist at Marshfield Clinic who specialized in the disease and had many patients with it.

I told my doctor about him. She called and arranged a second opinion for me.

As Jim and I drove there a few days later, I was aware of how the disease was getting worse. I was having problems with swallowing, and I had double vision more each day.

When we met with this doctor, I felt he was my last hope. It turned out he would help me open up a new, positive chapter in my life.

He disagreed with the other neurologist. He wanted me to have thymectomy surgery as soon as possible. He had several past patients who had the surgery and whose symptoms were greatly improved.

He listened to my concerns, and I felt he really cared about me as a person. He would become a major part of my medical life for the next several years.

We went after the appointment to visit my parents and tell them about the situation. The surgery would be scheduled at the beginning of June—the last day of school.

Preparing myself mentally for this major surgery was my next task. When you have major surgery, you are forced to face your own mortality. It is a scary experience.

The night before the surgery, I called all of my brothers and sisters and talked to them. I ended my conversations with "I love you," which wasn't something I typically did. I didn't want to miss the opportunity to say it.

Jim said goodnight to me and left for the evening. He told me he would have the phone next to his bed if I needed to call him and talk. I was trying to be brave, and I told him everything would be all right. But inside, I was very worried.

Before I went to bed, I went in the bathroom and looked in the mirror. I stared at my image and traced with my finger starting at the top of my breastbone. I imagined what was going to be happening tomorrow. I looked at my old self in the mirror and hoped that after tomorrow's surgery, my life would start going in a new direction—a better one.

That night, I didn't get any sleep; my anxieties were catching up with me. It was two in the morning when I called Jim. He came over right away.

I was a pathetic mess. We laid on the floor together the rest of night. I cried and he held me. His strength helped the long night pass more quickly.

I would need his strength in the days to come.

Chapter Ten

It's All a Blur

Sorrow looks back, worry looks around, faith looks up.

—*Anonymous*

The scene was right out of an old slapstick comedy. There I was lying on a gurney, wearing the standard hospital gown that reveals much more than most people feel comfortable with, and a young intern was wheeling me through a series of narrow hallways. Crash! I recognized the sound of broken glass.

An expletive was uttered under his breath. Whatever machine was knocked over, I hoped it wasn't needed today—especially for me.

I was actually relieved to get to the surgery room. It was smaller than I expected. I was asked to climb onto the operating table, which was surprisingly narrow.

As I was prepared for surgery, my gown was opened up and what looked like iodine was slathered on my chest. Thymectomy surgery requires the same incision as open-heart surgery. The chest is cut, the breastbone is cracked open, and the ribs are spread to give the surgeon access to the thymus gland.

The intern was looking at my chart. "So this is her second thymectomy?"

"Can't be," replied a nurse. "Look at her chest. There isn't any scar."

"But it says on here it's her second one …"

I was really starting to get nervous now. Then a voice of reason spoke up. It was my surgeon.

"This is her first thymectomy," he said. He saw the concern on my face. "Relax, Sheila. It will be fine."

Despite my best efforts to fight it, the medication I had been given to relax me was taking effect. But before I gave in to it, I turned to the intern, grabbed his shirt, and pulled myself up to his face.

"It does say *thymectomy* on that chart, right?" I asked.

Looking back, I think my desperation was probably a little intimidating to him.

"Yes, it does say thymectomy …"

The next thing I remember was seeing bright lights. Blinking my eyes, I tried to reorient myself with my surroundings.

Did I die? Is this heaven?

I turned my head, only to see people lined up as far as I could see, lying on tables. I turned my head the other way, only to see the same thing.

"She is awake," a voice said. "Close your eyes, dear."

I did as I was told. My next memory involved the sound of familiar voices and the shadowy images of loved ones. The ICU was very dark, and I distinctly recall having an incredible thirst.

Jim fed me ice chips while many family members looked on. There were jokes and stories to take my mind off of my ordeal—or maybe to occupy everyone else's thoughts.

Jim stayed with me until early in the morning. I can remember the sounds of gagging and vomiting from other patients nearby. My sense of hearing seemed almost hypersensitive, and I kept asking Jim to talk to me so we didn't hear that awful sound.

There was a wonderful nurse who helped me that night, and I kept looking at her name badge, struggling to remember her name. Although her name is forgotten, her compassion is not.

For the next day, it seemed as though I was having an out-of-body experience. The weakness I felt was incredible. It was almost as if I was watching myself from a far corner of a room, observing the pitiful spectacle I had become.

The pain in my chest was indescribable. It felt like a knife cutting skin, and there was a distinct burning sensation. The incision was about eight inches long, and the swelling of the muscles made it so that if I looked down, my chin could almost touch the top of the incision.

The surgery was considered a success. My thymus gland, normally the size of the end of an adult pinkie at thirty years old, was over three inches long and an inch-and-a-half thick. Pathology would show that it was filled with myasthenia antibodies. Its removal was essential.

The night before the surgery, I'd had a conversation with God. I begged him for mercy, pleading that He would allow me to live through this experience.

A few days later, I would be praying again, asking for the pain to end.

Chapter Eleven

In Another's Hands

Each handicap is like a hurdle in a steeplechase. When you ride up to it, if your throw your heart over, the horse will go along, too.

—Lawrence Bixby

The first few days after the surgery were a humbling experience. When you have major surgery, you discover quickly how you end up putting your life in the hands of others. Doctors and nurses are an incredible group of people. They typically deal with very unhappy patients who are usually in a great deal of pain.

However, it should be noted that they are people, and people do make mistakes. That was something I would learn firsthand.

The second evening I was in the hospital, I had a taste of what real pain feels like. Every two to three hours, someone would check on me. At around midnight, the night nurse stopped in and changed the morphine drip bag. Within the next hour, I started to have a significant increase in pain. I pressed the button, and a different nurse came in. I explained my symptoms and asked if she could check the bag. She smiled, glanced at the equipment, and said I was fine.

Throughout the night, the pain continued to increase. At around seven in the morning, a new nurse started her shift. I had buzzed three times in the night and complained but to no avail. When the new nurse arrived, she came in with a doctor. Apparently, it was noted in my chart that I'd had a difficult evening. By this time, the pain was indescribable.

I explained to both of them what I was feeling—a burning sensation in my chest that seemed to get worse by the minute. The doctor looked more carefully at my pain machine and let out a small gasp. He pressed some buttons, grabbed the nurse's arm, and led her out of the room.

When he returned a few minutes later, he looked visibly concerned.

"I am so sorry," he apologized. "Your machine for your morphine drip was turned off when the bag was replaced."

I had been without morphine for seven hours. No wonder I hurt so much!

The lesson I learned was a valuable one. Don't ever give up on letting medical personnel know how you feel.

By the third day, I was taken off the morphine, and my chest tubes were removed. The chest tubes had been the most painful part of the experience so far. Every time I would breathe in and out, it felt like a knife cutting through skin. I was never so thankful as I was when those tubes were removed.

I was released from the hospital five days after my surgery. I was anxious to get home but worried as to how it would feel. My sister Colleen stayed with Jim and I to help me for the first few days. I was so thankful to have her there.

I was taking only Tylenol with codeine for my pain, which was not helpful at all. I was using a pillow to hug against my chest whenever I needed to cough. Moving around was vital for my health but extremely difficult because of the constant pain I was in.

After the third day home, I started to have a different type of pain in a different part of my body. My back started having stabbing pains right below the backside of my rib cage. I thought that maybe I had pulled a muscle in my back. As each hour passed, the pain increased.

I found myself crying because I was so miserable and in such agony. I remember going to the emergency room of our local hospital and being examined by an ER doctor who informed me I needed Vicodin to help me with the pain since I obviously wasn't handling it well.

I felt depressed and ashamed that I couldn't stand the pain. I took the pills when we got back to the apartment and laid down to rest. I hadn't slept for more than an hour at a time in days.

Jim sat next to the bed with an icepack against my back and side, holding it there for over six hours without moving. When I woke up, the pain was worse than ever.

I didn't want to go back to the hospital. I didn't want to face anyone to let them know what or how I was feeling. I felt guilt over not being strong enough to physically withstand it.

Jim insisted we return to the hospital where my surgery was performed. It was an hour away, but he felt we had no choice.

We called my parents at four in the morning and met them there at the ER. By this point, I was delirious and on the verge of passing out.

A doctor entered the examination room and proceeded to look me over. He was surrounded by a group of interns. This was a teaching hospital, and I was an interesting case.

Tests were run, and within twenty minutes, they had discovered what was happening. Pulmonary embolism—blood clots in both of my lungs.

I was lucky that Jim got me there when he did. It was a close call.

Chapter Twelve

An Attempt at Normalcy

A successful marriage is an edifice that must be rebuilt every day.

—*André Maurois*

For the next eight days, I found myself in a different part of the hospital. Instead of being in the heart surgery area, I was now in with the "general" cases. There were fewer nurses and many more interns practicing on their patients.

I found out quickly that it is not good to have small, moving veins. Blood withdrawals every two hours left me with an arm covered in bruises from the wrist past the elbow. Eventually, I ended up with what are known as "blown veins," and to this day phlebotomists still have a hard time finding any veins on my right arm that are usable.

I was given a drug called heparin and later was put on Coumadin; both drugs are blood thinners. I had several tests, including one I think was called a pulmonary ventilation/perfusion scan.

The trauma of staying in a hospital for so many days was starting to get to me. So were the interns. They were like a flock of birds, swooping in during any time of the day, surrounding my bed, all asking me the same questions. I was tired of being a medical freak show. I wanted to go home, start preparing for our wedding at the end of July, and get my life back to normal again.

I remember my parents visiting me in the hospital and staying for most of the day, every day I was there. Jim would come in the evenings after work and sit with me.

One day I stood beside my bed looking out the window with Jim, watching my parents leave the hospital, and I was overcome with a feeling I have never had before or since. I think it would probably be called a panic attack, but I was really convinced that I would never leave that hospital. I told Jim my feelings, and he talked to a nurse and made arrangements to have us go and sit outside.

It was the greatest relief to sit outside, smell fresh air, and feel that it was possible to return to something that slightly resembled normalcy. It was the happiest I had been in a long time.

After all the tests and all the pain, I was finally released from the hospital. The urge to get out of there was soon replaced by the fear of returning. After everything that had gone wrong, I was worried about what the future held.

I had a month to recuperate and get ready for our wedding day. The plans for the wedding had kept me going during all of this. I was so excited to finally get married and start sharing my life with Jim.

On our wedding day, one of my friends came over to my apartment and put on my makeup. Later that morning, we packed up the car and headed for the church. I remember walking around the church in my shorts and T-shirt, totally relaxed, when the priest walked up to me and asked when I was going to get dressed. I figured that was more than a subtle hint that I needed to prepare.

As my mom and I started to get me into the wedding dress, we looked for the veil, and that's when we realized—it was gone. Earlier that day, I had taken it out of the bag with the dress and put it on to see how I looked with the makeup. My apartment was across town, and the wedding was to start in twenty minutes.

My sister and sister-in-law raced across town to get the veil while my friends played an extra twenty minutes of music in between. Forgetting my veil turned out to be the only thing that went wrong that day. And considering everything that had led up to that moment, it was a very small detail—but one that family members and friends who were there that day look back on with a smile.

Our wedding day was a very special moment in our lives. When we looked into each other's eyes during our vows, "in sickness and in health" took on a whole new dimension. We had been through a lot just in the short time we were engaged.

It was a day filled with precious moments. It was a day I will never forget. But marriage is more than just a ceremony and a reception. It is a lifetime commitment that requires work. That is something only time and experience can teach you.

Chapter Thirteen

Part of the Plan

There are only two ways to live your life. One is as though nothing is a miracle. The other is as though everything is a miracle.

—Albert Einstein

Some people may call it coincidence, while others would point to divine intervention. I have evolved over the years from believing that circumstances occur randomly without reason to believing that God has a plan for all of us.

When I became pregnant with Michael, it was literally a miracle. My previous health problems combined with uterine fibroids made the prospect of having a child unlikely. And even though I had dreamed about having a family, after the myasthenia gravis diagnosis, we were told to wait for three years after surgery and then see how it went.

Statistics say that about one third of pregnant MG patients see a relapse or worsening of their symptoms, and about two thirds of patients see a lessening of their symptoms or even go into remission.

Before I became pregnant, I was so focused on maintaining my own health that after the three years were up, I almost started to panic. I was doing well, and I really was worried about risking it, but Jim was anxious to start a family. We weren't getting any younger, and when I visited an OB-GYN for advice, he reminded me of that right away. He also suggested that the fibroids might become an issue but not to let that stop us.

At the same time I was going through my pregnancy, my parents were going through some changes themselves. My father's memory issues had become worse. One sign of this that I recognized was the decreasing length of our telephone conversations.

For years, conversations with my father had lasted on average about an hour. We would usually talk two to three times a week. My father was a great conversationalist and was fluent in many topics. During the course of a typical telephone conversation, we could talk about current events, the weather, politics, and sports, just to name a few topics. But as his memory issues increased, it became apparent that there was more going on than just old age setting in. Eventually those long, thoughtful exchanges trailed off to a matter of minutes, with my dad surrendering the phone to my mom because of his lack of coherent thoughts.

My interactions with my parents became limited during this time by the complications I had during the last trimester. One summer day, I started having severe abdominal pains and had to be hospitalized. Tests were done to see if I was in labor. My pains were so strong that they were registering as contractions. Luckily that was not the case, but I was initially diagnosed with an ulcer and given Protonix. Unfortunately, throughout the course of my pregnancy I was to learn what the different classes of prescription drugs were.

I returned a few weeks later with more severe pains. A morphine drip was administered, and I was told upfront by my doctor that I had to take painkillers to control my pain. Ultrasounds indicated that as the baby was growing, so were the fibroids. The pain was so intense that if I didn't take medication to control it, I would end up right back in the hospital.

One fibroid in particular was protruding from my belly-button area. I could literally press on it and observe its reaction. I decided to name that fibroid Fred, since we seemed to have such a personal relationship. Laughing at the situation seemed better than crying.

Still, I can honestly say I did a lot more crying during those months than laughing. Fortunately, I had a supportive husband, family, and friends who did everything they could to help me cope with everyday life.

Evenings during the last month were the worst. I couldn't sleep lying down, so I slept in an easy chair in the living room. I was anxious to meet our new child. We didn't want to know the sex of the child before it was born. Jim was convinced that it was a girl, and I was convinced the opposite.

A few days before the birth, we had stopped in to visit one of my coworkers whose daughter was due to have her baby the day before us. Tragically, earlier in the day her daughter had lost the baby at birth and was herself in critical condition in the hospital. My heart was crushed. Life is so fragile, and this was a personal reminder.

Three days later, my turn came. When I went into labor, I was terrified. As anyone who has had a baby can attest, there is nothing like it. As our child was about to be born, a neurologist was also present to make sure that the baby did not have postnatal MG. All of the people, all of the faces—I just tried to focus on Jim and my doctor as they coached me through it all.

I was grateful that the labor was only about twelve hours long, and for me the epidural provided much-needed relief. But of all the experiences during that whole process, the greatest was the very end—that is, the end of my labor and the beginning of our son's life.

The moment of his birth was truly miraculous. "It's a boy," my doctor announced, and our newborn son filled the room with his piercing cry. He was immediately checked out and proclaimed healthy by the medical staff.

As my husband handed Michael over to me, I said, "Hey, Michael, what are you crying about?"

He stopped crying, turned his head, and looked straight into my eyes. For that brief moment, I felt a divine presence. I felt closer to God than at any other time in my life. A wonderful feeling of peace surrounded me, and I was without any pain.

Just as my son Michael had entered my life, my father—at least, the person I knew and loved—was slowly leaving it. It is interesting how God weaves his plan.

Chapter Fourteen

The Longest Good-bye

Great opportunities to help others seldom come,
but small ones surround us daily.

—*Sally Koch*

I tried to use the clock on the wall as a distraction. The second hand was obviously broken, as it repeatedly twitched and the clock perpetually stayed at 11:55. *How ironic*, I thought. *Time is literally standing still. I wonder if that is what it feels like for him?*

The nurse had been finishing up feeding my dad his lunch when I walked in. I was nervous about visiting him by myself. I'd always had my mother with me. I didn't know if he would recognize me. My worst fears were realized. He didn't.

"Look, Pat. Your daughter is here to see you," the nurse stated in a kind voice.

He looked at me with confused eyes. "I don't know her," he mumbled.

"I'll wait in the hallway until you are done," I told the nurse.

"Don't worry about it. We're finished up here."

At that moment I longed for my mom—the type of longing you have as a child, seeking protection from the unknown. I tried to convince myself that this was a good idea.

The television was blaring an old country-western variety show. I tried to turn down the volume. I didn't think that my dad would mind. He actually couldn't stand country music, and I knew that if he'd had control over the situation, he would have found CNN or something similar to watch instead.

When my mom and I would visit Dad, there would be periods of silence, but somehow it didn't seem to bother me so much. She would just sit there, holding his hand. Sometimes she would pull out a brush from her purse and gently comb his hair.

Today, I had decided to be brave and come alone. It was a two-hour drive from our home, and on the way there, I tried to think up one-sided conversations that would work.

Dementia changes your life in ways you could never imagine.

I pulled up a chair next to my dad and took his hand. What would Mom do? I smiled and gently stroked his hand. His eyes changed, and he smiled.

Our moment of solitude was interrupted by a voice.

"There is a phone call for you, Sheila. You can take it at the front desk."

Jim was the only one who knew I was coming here today. What could it be? I hoped nothing serious had happened.

I went to pull my hand from my father's and met with a grip from which I could not escape.

"No ... no ... don't go," he pleaded. His strength was almost frightening. Here was a man who was bedridden, yet his hands were just as powerful as when they were working on our farm.

"It's okay, Dad. I'll be right back," I reassured him.

When I got to the front desk, I discovered it was my sister Colleen on the phone. She had called our house in the morning after I had left and wondered if she could come over with Mom to join our visit. My mother had been living with my sister and brother-in-law for several months now.

My father had been placed in hospice several months earlier and was one of the few people I had ever known who actually got out of the program alive.

I returned to the room to find him sitting up in bed, staring out of the window. I pulled a small book out of my purse. It was a compilation of poetry by Robert Frost, my father's favorite.

My dad's favorite poem was *The Road Not Taken*. I started to read it and occasionally glanced at him to see if he was listening. He kept staring outside, so I concentrated on the poem.

I shall be telling this with a sigh
Somewhere ages and ages hence:
Two roads diverged in a wood, and I—
I took the one less traveled by,
And that has made all the difference.

I finished the poem and looked up at him. The confusion in his eyes had been replaced by recognition, and as tears rolled down his cheeks and filled mine, I wondered if sometimes in such situations not knowing your surroundings was a blessing.

Chapter Fifteen

Hope Never Ends

If ye have faith as small as a grain of mustard seed ...
Nothing shall be impossible unto you.

—Matthew 17:20

I can't stand the smell of those places. I had enough experiences with hospitals to know that no matter how much you tried to ignore it, it was still a building filled with very sick people, and that was one reality that no cleaning solution can ever fully disguise.

As we walked up to the room, I could see the door was partially open, and I could hear the distinct voices of three people inside. Lois's voice sounded the same as always—peppy and full of fun, even in a hospital setting.

I was ashamed to admit that I hadn't seen my friend for a few months that summer. I was busy taking care of my son, Michael, who would be turning one in September. The last time I had seen her was early in the summer, when she came over to our house for a visit. When she got out of the car, I couldn't believe how much her appearance had changed. She looked like she had lost at least forty pounds. But her spirit was the same.

Lois was one of those people who attracted friends. She was like a "friend magnet," while I, on the other hand, was more introverted by nature and had a difficult time opening up to people. Lois recognized that, but for some reason she liked what she saw in me and made an effort to be my friend.

When I was single, we spent time together playing golf, going to the movies, eating out, and sometimes just calling each other up and talking about our jobs.

In many ways, Lois was like a big sister to me and was in fact the same age as my sister Carol. We were very close, and that made watching her struggle against cancer even more difficult.

Lois was the first person in my life I knew so personally who had stage-four cancer. But you would never know it by talking with her. Her attitude was incredibly positive.

Death was not a topic of our conversations. Our focus was always on the future and her plans to be a part of that future.

We were visiting her that day to share with her pictures from our recent cruise to Alaska. Lois was a world traveler and had shared with us last fall how Alaska was one of her favorite places.

Lois and I both grew up on farms, and as children, traveling long distances was out of the question. Every summer for as long as I had known Lois, she traveled to someplace special. When school started again in the fall, she would be sure to bring pictures from her latest adventure to share with her fellow librarians. She was proud to let you know that she had visited every state in the union, and a visit to her home would provide you with an opportunity to look at the photos that lined her staircase, many of which chronicled her travels. I envied her outgoing nature and her sense of adventure.

As we went through the Alaska pictures, she eagerly described her experiences in many of the places we had visited. I had gotten better at ignoring the changes in her outward appearance. Her enthusiasm made you forget the seriousness of her situation.

As I look back on that afternoon, I am so happy that we took time from our busy lives to share that precious time together. As the next few months would prove, time is something you can't replace.

Chapter Sixteen

Best Friends

Fare thee well for I must leave thee,
Do not let this parting grieve thee,
Just remember that even the best of friends must part.

—Anonymous

The first time I went there, I didn't know what to expect. Visiting someone in a hospice house was a new experience for me. It was definitely a more inviting atmosphere than a hospital setting.

I rang the doorbell and was greeted by a friendly volunteer who asked me the name of the person I was visiting. She led me through the home. It had rooms like you would find when you entered someone's house—a living room, a kitchen, and several bedrooms that were offshoots of the main rooms of the house.

I had a strange feeling when I walked into Lois's room. Throughout her battle with cancer, I had honestly never believed she would get to this point. Her obvious love for life and everything it had to offer would help her get through anything, or so I thought. Now she was at the point of no return: hospice.

Yet even when I saw her there, sitting straight up in her bed, her big bright eyes smiling at me, she was saying, "Hey girl! How are you? Come on in!" I still couldn't believe how upbeat she was.

Her room had several chairs, a large television, and a beautiful picture window that looked out at trees with a bird feeder. Photographs, cards, and many other reminders of family and friends surrounded her. Perhaps most importantly, she was surrounded by people. Lois loved people, and I think their presence provided her with the much-needed comfort she deserved during that difficult time.

Looking back, I often wished there was a time when I visited her that we could have been alone, just the two of us, so I'd have had the opportunity to let her know how important she was to me and how much I cared. But that wasn't part of God's plan. Maybe that was a good thing. God knows I am an oversensitive spirit, and it would have been too difficult for both of us.

We would instead spend our last days together talking about the future—my future. I had recently accepted the position of school librarian at a new elementary school being built in our district. Our discussions involved plans I was making for the new library: collection development, floor plans, furniture, and so on.

One day, she asked me to bring in copies of the lesson plans that I used with fifth-graders. I was surprised, wondering why she would want to see them. After all, teaching was not a possibility for her anymore. But not wanting to offend her, I did as she requested, returning the next day with a folder containing what she had asked of me.

I will always remember her scanning the papers, resting the folder on her grossly enlarged stomach—a stomach distended by the ever-growing tumor that was slowly taking her away from us. Her eyes grew weary, and she winced in pain.

She turned to me and said, "Sometimes it is just too much, Sheila."

I nodded and smiled. I took her hand in mine and gently squeezed it.

It was the only time I ever saw even a moment of discouragement. Then, as quickly as the moment had come, it disappeared. She literally shook her head, as if to physically remove the doubts themselves, and smiled back at me.

"Oh well. Tomorrow is another day, Sheila. Tomorrow is another day."

The next day when I visited Lois, I brought my friend Marie with me. When we walked in the room, Lois was lying on her side, now wearing an oxygen tube, with her hands cupped together under her head. She looked like a small child, sleeping peacefully. Her niece, Annette, who had been a constant family presence throughout this ordeal, was sitting by her side.

"Last night was a rough one," she told us.

We stayed and talked to Annette for quite a while. She shared how Lois looked over my lesson plans more thoroughly after I had left the day before.

Annette said with a tender smile, "She told me to tell you that the lessons look good. She said 'Sheila knows what she is doing.'" I smiled in return.

As we left that day, another friend was coming through the door. Lois was blessed with many friends.

The next day was Thanksgiving, and when I called Annette, she said the family had decided to just have family members only visit from this point on. The end was near.

Throughout the long weekend, I waited for a call from friends. Nothing happened.

When I returned to work the following Monday, at recess break, in the lounge, some of my coworkers were discussing the situation and asked if I had heard any news. I had not.

After the bell rang, I went out into the hallway and met my principal there. The look on his face said it all.

"Sheila, I just heard that Lois passed away earlier this morning. I wanted to tell you in person, since I know that you were such good friends."

The news shouldn't have shocked me, but it actually did. The finality of it was surprisingly stunning.

With tears in my eyes, I excused myself and slowly walked up the stairs. I walked into the back room of the library and splashed water on my face. Within minutes, I would have a class of second-graders walking into the library, and I needed to compose myself.

As I left the back room and was greeted by cheerful young students, I noticed my principal walking up to me. He offered to teach my class if I needed it. That was very thoughtful of him, but I graciously declined.

I could hear Lois's voice in my head: "The show must go on, girl!"

And so it did.

Chapter Seventeen

Reality Strikes

*God made the world round so we would never
be able to see too far down the road.*

—Isak Dinesen

There were many changes taking place in my life. I was spending long hours working on plans for my new job. Developing a library from the ground up was a once-in-a-lifetime opportunity, and now I was using my past experience and education to help me make that dream come true.

My family was happy for me but also concerned about the stress involved and how it would impact my health. To be honest, I was, too; looking back, I should have thought about that more before I tried for the job.

In my heart, I was happy where I was working. I had developed a great library program, and I had many wonderful friends who I hated to leave behind. In the past, there had been other job opportunities that came along, and I never took advantage of any of them for the same reason. Some may have seen those missed opportunities as a sign of complacency; I always saw them in a more positive light. I really liked what I did and didn't see why I should change just to "move up" the career ladder.

When I finally did make the leap, it might have appeared to be a positive sign of forward movement and ambition, but it just brought more pressure, stress, and the return of symptoms I hadn't seen for several years.

These concerns led me, in February of 2006, to make the hardest decision I had ever made in my career. I stepped down from the job.

It was the first time in my life that I quit something that I was so passionate about. I just couldn't see myself continuing down that road and maintaining the health I had worked so hard to attain.

That spring, my health continued to spiral downward. In March, I had an infection that left me with a fever of 103 degrees and a rash over my entire body from a drug reaction to sulfur. Three weeks later, I came down with a strep throat infection that presented new and disturbing symptoms.

It started when I began the antibiotic for the strep infection. I felt the effects only hours after taking the first pill. The thumb on my right hand felt like it was tingling and numb. By the next day, the sensation had spread to my entire hand and up my arm. It was the weekend, and I went back to the walk-in clinic on Sunday, getting a different doctor with a different opinion. He switched medications, but the symptoms continued to spread to my other arm and feet. I was having blurred vision. I felt like my body was on full alert and attacking me constantly.

I returned to my neurologist, and he examined me and assured me it was not MG—but he didn't know what it *was*. All I knew was it was getting worse, and my entire body felt like it was battling a very bad case of the influenza.

I will spare you the details of the number of doctor visits I went through, specialists I saw, and questions that could not be answered. I was already a medical rarity, and these new symptoms only left me feeling helpless all over again.

No one had any answers, and I needed some direction to go in. The pain was different from anything I had experienced before. It was all throughout my body.

I asked for a second opinion, this time from the Mayo Clinic in Rochester, Minnesota. My experience there was unlike anything I'd had previously.

I would recommend the Mayo Clinic to anyone. It is the definition of precision and excellence in health care. I went through three days of grueling tests and a rigid schedule. Even though it is a huge institution, all of the people I encountered were friendly and thoughtful.

The neurologist who was assigned to my case spent the first twenty minutes of my patient interview questioning me about depression and its effects on my symptoms. It was only after he gave me a physical exam that he seemed to take my concerns more seriously.

Jim stayed at home with Michael during my visit to Mayo, but my sister Carol graciously gave up time from her job and family to take me to the clinic. Even though this was an extremely stressful time in my life, it was also a wonderful opportunity to spend time with my sister. Family support is essential during tough times.

The Mayo Clinic concluded I had fibromyalgia, defined on mayoclinic. com as:

> A chronic condition characterized by widespread pain in your muscles, ligaments and tendons, as well as fatigue and multiple tender points—places on your body where slight pressure causes pain.... Signs and symptoms of fibromyalgia can vary, depending on the weather, stress, physical activity or even the time of day.

The pain associated with fibromyalgia is described as a constant dull ache, typically arising from muscles. To be considered widespread, the pain must occur on both sides of your body and above and below your waist.

> Fibromyalgia is characterized by additional pain when firm pressure is applied to specific areas of your body, called tender points. Tender point locations include:

- Back of the head

- Between shoulder blades

- Top of shoulders

- Front sides of neck

- Upper chest

- Outer elbows

- Upper hips

- Sides of hips

- Inner knees

There are eighteen trigger points associated with fibromyalgia and I had sixteen of them identified by the neurologist during his exam.

I had the answers I was seeking. Before I could find out how that development was going to shape our future, an unexpected tragedy put things into perspective.

Chapter Eighteen

My Father-in-Law, My Friend

The question is not whether we will die but how we will live.

—Joan Borysenko

It began like any other typical March day in Wisconsin. It was cold, and there was a light snow in the air. It was a Tuesday, which meant I was at one of my rural schools for the day. Looking back at my teaching diary, I note that my classes went very smoothly, and I was pleased with how my library lessons were received by my students. I had started working with the fifth-grade students and their teacher on a computer project in the lab.

The phone rang in the early afternoon, and when I picked it up, I barely recognized the voice on the other end of the line. It was my husband.

"Sheila? Dad died ..." he said, and then he began to sob.

"He died?" I was in shock. We had just had supper with Jim's parents a few days earlier.

Jim gave me the details of how his parents were grocery shopping in the morning, and how his father collapsed at the checkout counter and died of a massive heart attack. He told me which hospital emergency room they were at. I told him I would get there as soon as I could and hung up the phone. I turned to my assistant.

"Are you okay?" she asked. I'm sure the look on my face reflected the obvious loss I was feeling.

"My father-in-law died this morning." The words seemed unreal, even though I heard my own voice speak them.

51

"Come with me," she said as she gently took my hand, and we went into the back room of the library. Once she closed the door, she turned to me and embraced me. She held me tight and whispered beautiful prayers that comforted my soul.

There are specific moments of grace that every person experiences in his or her life. This was one of those moments, and I am so grateful God had us working together during that very difficult time in my life.

I let the office know why I had to leave. As I drove to the hospital, the snow was coming down harder. I didn't know what to expect when I got there.

When I walked into the room, the first thing I noticed was the sounds. I guess it could best be described as soft cries. My father-in-law was lying on a gurney, wrapped in a white sheet, his mouth slightly open with a respirator tube sticking out. My husband was holding his hand and kneeling next to him. My mother-in-law kept repeating out loud, "I can't believe he is gone. I can't believe this ..."

None of us could believe it. The nurse walked in and explained to us that Gene had died within a matter of minutes, and that even though the situation was agonizing for all of us, he died as quickly and as relatively painlessly as a person can.

Later that afternoon, we returned to my in-laws home. I glanced around the house and noticed all of the little things that usually go unnoticed on a normal day. Change left on top of the refrigerator, a jacket on a kitchen chair, an unfinished jigsaw puzzle on the dining-room table—normally insignificant items that now seemed valuable in a very personal way.

That evening was a very long and difficult one. As I lay awake, I remembered my father-in-law fondly—a quiet man of few words, but when he did speak, you listened intently as he shared stories of his past. Throughout the years I knew him, he shared with me details about how he had designed and built their home. He was a very skilled mason. He also loved to read, and Westerns were among his favorites.

He loved fishing and spending summers vacationing in northern Wisconsin. His musical passion was jazz, and my in-laws' home was usually filled with the pleasant sounds of jazz in the background.

But I believe by far his greatest love in life was his family. He was a very devoted husband, father, and grandfather.

One of my personal favorite memories of Gene took place on my wedding day. At the reception, I can remember him gently taking my hand

and leading me out onto the dance floor. A few moments after the music began and we started to dance, he looked at me and smiled.

"You don't know how to dance, dear, do you?" he said.

"No, not at all," I admitted. We both had a good laugh. Then he said, "Don't worry. Just follow my lead and do your best."

Looking back at that time in our lives, it was very challenging for all of us. But I believe that one of Gene's favorite authors, Louis L'Amour, said it best when he wrote, "There will come a time when you believe that everything is finished. Yet that will be the beginning …"

I was very fortunate to have known Gene and to have had him as both my father-in-law and my friend.

Chapter Nineteen

Reflections of Joy

God hath made me to laugh, so that all that hear will laugh with me.

—Genesis 21: 6

What brings joy to my life? When I stop to really think about it, I am fortunate to find that my answer gets longer and better with age.

First and foremost is my family, right at the top of the list. I have been blessed with a very supportive and loving family—parents who supported me through everything, a husband who loves me unconditionally, and a son who inspires me with his kind heart. My siblings and their spouses embrace me, my nephews and nieces respect me, and my in-laws have treated me as if I have always been a part of their family since the beginning. I can't imagine a better family.

I am a firm believer in trying to live a life that is balanced. Every day we find ourselves pulled in so many different directions, and whenever we become too absorbed in one area of our lives, we risk finding ourselves out of balance. I am the first to admit that I have become obsessed at certain times in my life with my career, my health, or my relationships. Anytime that happened, I suffered as a result, and so did those who love me.

When your health is far from perfect, you do find yourself thinking about it quite often. I think that is only natural. The key is to refocus your thoughts. I find myself doing that several times a day. For me, prayer and meditation are important. Setting aside a few moments, especially in the morning, for quiet time, prayers, and writing helps me to generate positive thoughts and get my day started on the right foot.

When difficult times pop up during the day, deep cleansing breathing and short prayers do wonders to renew the soul. Positive thinking is also vital. Every day, I read something from Norman Vincent Peale. His thoughts, supported by Bible verses, are very encouraging.

Since I tend to tilt toward pessimism, surrounding myself with positive people helps me tremendously. I have always been attracted to upbeat people, especially those with a great sense of humor. There is nothing like a good belly laugh.

Life is made up of precious moments that go beyond the milestones we commonly think about. For me, those moments include the sound of my son's laugh; getting "huggie attacks" from Michael as I climb the stairs after a long day at work; playing tag and rolling around on the grass on a summer's day; cooking meals with my mom; curling up with a good book and a warm blanket, drinking a hot cup of tea; finishing a pencil sketch; talking with a friend I haven't seen in a long time; watching a classic comedy with Jim and laughing until our eyes water; the silent sounds of fishing; going golfing with friends; watching a Packer game (when they are winning!) …

When life throws you a curve ball, when you find yourself lying in a hospital bed struggling to feel normal again, those are the thoughts that get you through the night.

I'm sure if you stop right now and think about all of the so-called little things in life that bring you joy, your own list would be longer than you think. I urge you to take a few moments each day to thank God for all those precious moments. I know I do.

Chapter Twenty

Christmas 2007

The Little Ship

I stood watching as the little ship sailed out to sea. The setting sun tinted his white sails with a golden light, and as he disappeared from sight a voice at my side whispered, "He is gone."

But the sea was a narrow one. On the farther shore a little band of friends had gathered to watch and wait in happy expectation. Suddenly they caught sight of the tiny sail and, at the very moment when my companion had whispered, "He is gone," a glad shout went up in joyous welcome: "Here he comes!"

-Author Unknown

It was Christmas 2007. It was our first Christmas without my father-in-law, and the holiday was filled with bittersweet moments. Michael was at that age where every experience was new and exciting.

The day went quite well—we ate wonderful food, shared good stories, played a board game, and relaxed in front of the tree. Michael fell asleep in my arms in the rocking chair. Jim's family had left to go home, and Jim decided to lie down to take a nap.

My thoughts turned to Christmases past and the joy that they brought to my childhood. As I rocked Michael alone in the living room, I started to cry. I missed my parents and thought about how my dad was spending this Christmas day lying in a bed in a nursing home dealing with dementia while my mom and brother were there doing their best to console him.

Early the next morning, we received a phone call. It was my brother Pat letting us know that my dad's health had taken a significant turn for the worse. I should come as soon as I could.

I grabbed some clothes and tried to prepare myself, both physically and mentally, for the journey ahead. There had been several close calls with my father over the past three years, but this time would be different. I could feel it.

I drove straight to the nursing home and, once there, headed to his room. One of the nurses recognized me in the hallway and told me my mom and brother had left for a few moments. She told me my dad had pneumonia, and that his respiration was getting weaker. It could be a matter of hours. Each patient was unique. Knowing my father, he would fight longer than most.

I entered his room, where a small lamp next to the bed provided the only light. A boom box was sitting on an end table playing soft classical music. The raspiness of my father's breathing was very noticeable.

As I sat beside his bed, my thoughts raced back to a conversation we'd had many years earlier regarding the death of his own mother. It was the first time I ever saw my father cry.

He recalled his mother's long drawn-out illness, and how at the very end, she was in a coma and unresponsive. He had found himself alone with her and realized he couldn't remember ever actually telling her the words *I love you*. So he leaned over her and whispered those words in her ear. She made a soft moaning sound in response.

With tears in his eyes, he asked me, "Do you think she heard me?"

"Yes, I'm sure she did. And even if she didn't, she knew it," I reassured him.

I have always believed that love is more than what you say, it is what you do. Words without actions are just empty. My father had lived a life filled with dedication to and love for his family and friends, and his parents saw that and knew that.

Now, nearly twenty-five years later, here I was in almost the same situation. The difference was, I did tell my dad those words throughout the years, especially the last few.

Even so, I took advantage of our time alone to softly talk to him, to let him know I was here and how much I cared.

There are some people on this earth you have a deep connection with. They complete your thoughts, understand your pain, share your joys, and relieve your anxieties. They support you during the good times and the bad. My father was more than a parent to me. He was also my therapist, my confidant, my hero, and my friend.

If you are lucky enough, you get to spend the majority of your life with someone like that. For me, my father was one of those people. And the next few hours would prove to be among the saddest and yet most profoundly moving of my life.

Chapter Twenty-One

In My Father's Eyes

*He was afraid and said, "How awesome is this place!
This is none other than the house of God; this is the gate of Heaven."*

—Genesis 28:17

As the hours passed, our family began to gather to be with our father during his death. My mother had been through so much with this disease, and I wondered if she comprehended the finality of these moments. I turned to her in the hallway as the staff moved Dad to another, more private room that would be larger for all of us to fit in. I grabbed her hand and squeezed it.

She looked deeply into my eyes and said, "This is such a sad day for our family, Sheila."

I knew she was preparing herself; we all were. Each of us had our own memories we were clinging to, our own joys, our own regrets—it all comes flooding into your mind in times like that.

My uncle Terry—my dad's only brother—and my aunt Hazel had arrived, followed closely by my sister Colleen. Their support and love had been a constant for my mother during this long journey that had started three years earlier.

My sister Carol had just had surgery recently and called my brother Pat on his cell phone. I could tell from the look on his face that her message was important. She wanted to be there, talk to dad, and say her good-byes.

My brother went into the room and talked to my dad, letting him know what Carol had told him.

Then late in the evening, Carol arrived with her husband, Joe. I will never forget her slowly walking into the lobby, determined to see our father. Despite obvious discomfort and pain, she rode several hours to sit by his side. Now she could relay her message personally.

It was late in the evening, and the nurses advised my mother to go home and get some rest. She would need her strength.

I honestly wondered if he would make it through the night. But my mother was convinced he would be there in the morning. She was right.

When we returned in the morning, Dad was still alive, still fighting. Meanwhile, as his condition worsened, so did the sounds he was emitting. Death from pneumonia is not a silent, painless process. With every struggling breath, he moaned louder. And despite the morphine, his painful cries could be heard from the hallway.

My brother Joe and his wife, Pauline, had the longest distance to travel. They called Pat in the morning and told him they were on their way. Soon all of our family would be together again one last time.

As the hours passed, we took turns comforting my father as best we could. It was a helpless feeling, knowing what was to come and yet praying for the suffering to end.

We tried to help him as best we could—putting cold washcloths on his forehead, rubbing his hands and legs, and of course, praying.

I must have whispered prayers a thousand times over. Many a *Lord have mercy* and *Christ have mercy*.

Then, within an hour of his death, my mother did the bravest thing I have ever witnessed. She gently placed her hands around his face, looked into his glassy eyes, and said, "Pat ... it's Marge. I want you to know it is okay to go. I will be fine, and I will see you soon."

Those in the room who also witnessed it will never forget that moment. When anyone since has asked me to define love, I tell him or her about that moment. There is no greater love than to let someone you love so dearly go.

When the moment of his death actually arrived, I don't remember exactly who was there or what was said. All I remember was what I saw.

My father let out a loud gasp, and my mother said, "He's leaving ... he's leaving ..." She reached out to him, and he raised himself ever so slightly.

And then I saw it—in his eyes. Those beautiful blue eyes that I was so familiar with had suddenly changed. Instead of being glassy and empty, as they had been so many times during this long journey, they were bright and full of hope. They sparkled as he saw something only he could see and yet we all could feel.

It was God. It was His beauty and strength. He had come to take Dad home.

Now when people ask me if I believe there is a God, I tell them I don't *believe* there is a God—I *know* there is one.

I saw Him in my father's eyes.

Chapter Twenty-Two

Divine Intervention

I know God will not give me anything I can't handle.
I just wish that He didn't trust me so much.

—*Mother Teresa*

As we drove to the church, my mother pointed out different buildings that had held some kind of significant place in my parents' past. Homes they had lived in before, parks they had picnicked in, businesses they had visited. My siblings who were with us on this trip acknowledged her memories because they remembered many of them also.

This was the town I was born in, but it was completely foreign to me. We had moved away when I was not even a year old, and the only time I visited it in later years was when we came to see my grandparents or attend weddings or funerals.

We had an appointment with the priest of my parents' former church. It was the church they attended as children and the one they were married in. Now it would serve its purpose one last time, as we gathered as a family to say good-bye to our father.

I must admit that when we walked up to the priest's home, I was a little bit nervous. When he opened the door, all of that nervousness disappeared. The man who opened the door and invited us in, the man who would oversee my father's funeral, could have easily won a lookalike contest. He looked like my father and, as he spoke, even sounded like him. I wondered if anyone else noticed.

As we all sat around the table together, the priest started to ask us questions about my father. It had been almost forty years since my parents had moved away from this community and this parish.

I handed over the two-page eulogy I had written for my dad. I asked the priest if he could possibly read it for me during the funeral. Father read it carefully, placed it back on the table, and slid it back toward me.

"I can't read this, Sheila," he replied politely.

I looked directly into his eyes. The experience was almost eerie. It was almost as if my dad were speaking himself.

"This is too personal. You must read it yourself or find someone in your family to read it for you."

A feeling came over me. I knew what I must do, but I wondered if I was capable of doing it. Public speaking was still not my favorite thing to do, let alone talking about someone who was as important to me personally as my dad.

As we drove home later, the discussion turned to who would be able to read the eulogy. I spoke up.

"I will do it," I said.

My siblings and my mother were concerned. They knew that stress was something I should avoid whenever possible. They were worried that this might be too much to ask.

I disagreed. I had made up my mind. I would do this—for my family and, maybe even more importantly, for me.

As we drove to the funeral a few days later, I kept from Jim my intention of reading the eulogy. Maybe I was afraid he might try to talk me out of doing it. I had practiced at home after Jim had gone to bed, sitting downstairs in our family room, reading it so that I could get through it without breaking down.

Surprisingly, I was not overcome with sadness when I saw my father in his coffin. He looked more like himself in death than he had for the last several months of his life. Much of the pain and suffering had been removed from his face. I was grateful he was finally at peace.

As people came into the church to give our family their condolences, I thought I saw a familiar face. My friend Cheryl walked up to me, and we embraced. I was so happy to see her, and her presence was very comforting.

The mass began, and I cannot recall most of it. The majority of the time I was concentrating on praying. I was trying to not focus on the finality of it all. This was my father's funeral—my father.

The priest nodded at me, and I nodded back. He knew I was ready to read the eulogy. As I walked past the coffin and stood in front of the church, I remembered my father's advice from my high school days—look at the back of the room, speak slowly, and take your time.

I read that eulogy. How did I do it? I can only say I believe it was divine intervention. My voice did not give out. My speech did not slur. I did not feel any numbness or tingling. I didn't even feel any pain. When I completed it, the only thing I did feel was pride.

I'm sure my Dad was looking down from heaven and smiling.

Chapter Twenty-Three

Memories of My Dad

The most beautiful things in the world are not seen nor touched.
They are felt with the heart.

—Helen Keller

This is the eulogy I delivered at my father's funeral:

How do you summarize eighty-two years of life on this earth? It is an impossible task, and so my goal is not to even try to do that. Instead, I would rather reflect on a life that was well-lived and on a person who was loved more than he ever knew.

Today is a day to remember—to cry, to laugh, but mostly to smile and celebrate a wonderful person who touched the lives of everyone in this church. Memories are something that make us uniquely human and are a great blessing. For some of us, we will be gently reminded of our father when we see a fishing pole and a tackle box filled with old fishing lures or the sound of waves gently striking a beach on Lake Superior. For others, it may be the smell of newly cut hay on a summer afternoon or the sight of an Allis Chalmers tractor slowly crossing a field. Maybe it will be entering a room filled with the hum of people enjoying conversations about politics and trading humorous stories. It could be something as simple as a bright orange hunting cap and a pair of bib overalls. Whatever sparks your memories, I am sure they are happy ones, filled with joy.

All of us have our own memories from which to draw.

My brothers and sisters will probably remember childhood summer visits to Hayward and our father's endless patience as he helped four children bait their hooks and untangle their fishing poles.

Maybe you will recall visits to our parents' cabin on Lake Superior, sitting around the kitchen table and playing Euchre until the wee hours of the morning.

Or the "debates" our father would have on any number of political, philosophical, and current-event topics.

Or perhaps your memories revolve around the serenity of fly-fishing on Bladder Lake in our Grandpa Fanning's old fishing boat.

My special memories involve words. All of the wonderful, long conversations I had with my father. It was from those conversations that I learned a great deal about my father and about our family history.

On October 24, 1925, in Milwaukee, Wisconsin, our father was born Patrick Cress Connors to two very loving and devoted parents, who most of us fondly remember as our grandparents, Eleanore and Joseph Connors. Our father grew up during the Great Depression, and it was from those humble beginnings that he learned from his parents very valuable traits he would have the remainder of his life—honesty, integrity, and perhaps most importantly, the belief that people should dedicate their lives to helping others.

Our father believed that you couldn't measure a man's wealth by how much money was in his bank account or how many material possessions he owned. Instead, our father believed that a man was truly wealthy if he had the love of his family and the loyalty of his friends. Using those standards, I am sure that you will agree when you look around this church today that our father was probably the richest man you will ever meet.

Our father was many things to many people. He was not only a father, grandfather, and great-grandfather, he was also a son, a brother, an uncle, an in-law, a cousin, a friend.

He was also a very dedicated and loving husband. Our parents were married fifty-nine years, and their devotion to each other, especially during times of crisis, was unmatched.

My parents taught me many lessons throughout my life. But perhaps the greatest lesson for me was the last one. During the final years of our father's life, he was stricken with dementia, a terrible disease that robs a person of that uniquely human trait—memory. When most people are given such a diagnosis, they react with fear and uncertainty. Instead, our parents faced this disease with dignity and courage. That is a valuable lesson for all of us. We may not be able to choose a disease that we are afflicted with, but we can choose how we react to that disease.

A few years ago, our dad gave me his prayer book that he took with him to church every Sunday. The book, old and worn, had a bookmark placed in his favorite spot. It was of a reading that is usually read at celebrations, such as weddings.

I think that today, as we celebrate his life, I will share with you that wonderful reading:

> Love is patient, love is kind. It does not envy, it does not boast, it is not proud. It is not rude, it is not self-seeking, it is not easily angered, it keeps no record of wrongs. Love does not delight in evil but rejoices with the truth. It always protects, always trusts, always hopes, always perseveres.
>
> Love never fails. But where there are prophecies, they will cease; where there are tongues, they will be stilled; where there is knowledge, it will pass away. For we know in part and we prophesy in part, but when perfection comes, the imperfect disappears. When I was a child, I talked like a child, I thought like a child, I reasoned like a child. When I became a man, I put childish ways behind me. Now we see but a poor reflection as in a mirror; then we shall see face to face. Now I know in part; then I shall know fully, even as I am fully known.
>
> And now these three remain: faith, hope and love. But the greatest of these is love.
>
> God Bless you Dad. We will miss you. May you rest in peace.

Chapter Twenty-Four

Regrets

Regret for the things we did can be tempered by time;
it is regret for the things we did not do that is inconsolable.

—*Sydney Harris*

One night, about six months after my father's death, I did something I will always regret. I yelled at my son.

You're only human, right? Everyone makes mistakes. True. But I have a tendency to let frustrations accumulate to a breaking point. Probably one of the reasons I have autoimmune disease. I let things fester to a point of no return.

My son, Michael, tends to be overly sensitive, both physically and emotionally. Just like his mother.

It was Sunday night, and I had returned earlier in the day from visiting my own mother, who was still dealing with her terrible loss. There were many emotions that I tried to contain and yet release at the same time. Michael is sensitive and picked up on that.

Lately, going to bed had been a difficult activity in our household. There were crying and delaying tactics, and the entire ordeal usually lasted around twenty minutes. But that night, it seemed to go on forever. First he needed one parent, then the other. It was becoming a game I didn't feel like playing anymore. So I yelled.

It was actually more like a primal scream. Built up inside of me was four years of guilt, anger, and anxiety. Guilt over having to take pain medication while I was pregnant with Michael. Anger that I didn't have the willpower to overcome the pain without pills. Anxiety that I had helped to create this overly sensitive child by the weakness of my actions.

I left his bedroom and, in despair, found myself downstairs, literally pounding the walls of our family room. Michael hysterically ran to our bedroom and was comforted by my husband.

Fifteen minutes later, Jim came downstairs. As I lay curled in a ball in my quilt, crying and asking for forgiveness from both God and my husband, there was an eerie silence between us.

"Why did you do that? Michael is never going to forget it."

I tried to explain all of the feelings I'd had for years that I couldn't seem to purge from my system.

All I could muster was, "I know he won't forget it. I'm sorry."

I won't forget either. I pray to God I won't ever forget.

Chapter Twenty-Five

The One That Got Away

Faith is a knowledge within the heart, beyond the reach of proof.

—Kahlil Gibran

My husband loves to fish, and it is when he is on the water, in our family fishing boat, searching for the trophy fish, that I see in him many of the qualities that attracted me when we first met ten years ago. All of the stresses of life—worries about money and bills, work pressures, anxiety about the future—all slip away, and he appears to be truly at peace with himself and his surroundings.

As I study him more closely, I notice the strength in his hands, the glistening of his tanned skin and the ease with which he casts and observes, waiting for the snap of the line and that joy of the moment where man and fish join in the ultimate battle.

My motive for fishing is much simpler and more selfish than his. I love to spend quiet time with Jim, where the only sounds you have to listen to are the reeling in of the line and the occasional plop of a fishing lure. We have had many quality conversations during our fishing expeditions, but sometimes the most enjoyable times have also been the most silent. Sometimes the stillness and peace of the moment gives people more of a connection than any words can describe.

One afternoon, I decided to pass up the opportunity to fish with Jim, and I instead chose to take a nap. My in-laws offered to watch our four-year-old son, and I was more than happy to enjoy some rest time.

Jim went out on the lake with a promise to return about an hour later. It was a very warm, humid day, and after I woke up from my nap, I sat up and started to read that elusive novel I had been meaning to get to for the last six months.

The afternoon slipped away quickly, and after the third hour, I started to really worry about him. I kept searching the horizon, looking for his silhouette to appear. Finally, I heard the familiar sound of our boat's motor and saw him approaching the dock. As I ran down to the boat to ask how his latest fishing adventure went, I could tell from the look on his face that he wasn't pleased.

"I lost the biggest fish of my life, Sheila." He described how he had caught a huge musky, and as he brought the fish up to the boat and tried to net it, the fish had broken away.

I could see the disappointment in his expression, and I could sense his frustration. Each time he talked to family members and friends over the next few days, he retold his story. Unlike some fishermen, Jim's tales do not become more exaggerated with time. One of his finest qualities is his honesty, and as you listened to him describe his quest to nab this huge fish, you could see and feel his honest regret at being unable to do so.

I tried to console Jim, but as I confessed earlier, I am not an expert fisherman. I did not have any answers as to why the fish got away. But it turned out that I didn't have to have any answers, because my husband's optimism, another one of those qualities I have always loved about him, resurfaced after the initial disappointment subsided.

As we watched our son playing with his cousins by the lakeshore, Jim and I discussed our many blessings, with Michael, our son, being at the top of the list. Listening to his endless chatter and the joy in his laughter, we held hands. With Jim's hand held firmly in mine, I was reminded once again of what is really important in life—and as it turns out, so was he.

Henry David Thoreau once said, "Many men go fishing all their lives without knowing it is not fish they are after." I wish that Jim could have actually caught that fish, but I was even happier to see that he recognized the blessings and love that surrounds us all.

Chapter Twenty-Six

It's All in the View

We are disturbed not by things, but by the view which we take of them.

—Epictetus

Some days are just fantastic and others … well, you just wonder, what is the point?

When chronic pain is a daily occurrence, negative thoughts can naturally get in the way of living a life that is full and has purpose.

What helps me get through the tough times? Where do I turn when I'm feeling discouraged? I simply turn to the one place that no matter what is going on—positive, negative, or indifferent—never changes, and that is my faith.

In my loneliest, darkest moments, I turn to my faith in God to find comfort. He is always with me, and just that simple understanding helps me to better cope with the stresses of everyday life.

Some people accept life. Some people fight it. I am, unfortunately, in the fighting category more than the acceptance one.

I want to control situations, because then I feel, even if it is not really true, that I can change anything if I really put my mind to it. However, the older I get, the more I am beginning to accept that this belief is not necessarily true.

Once, Jim and I were goofing off in the kitchen, and he wrapped his arms around me and lifted me completely off the floor. The feeling I had was of complete and utter fear. I was shocked by the way this small act of playfulness revealed such a huge weakness on my part. The sensation of literally being swept off my feet actually was unpleasant, because it represented how fearful I was of losing control over any aspect of my life, even the smallest ones.

Since that experience a few years ago, I have changed. I have learned that it is easier to face life's challenges if you accept what you can and can't control.

As time flies by, the more apparent it is to me that the only thing I really can control is my reaction to what happens to me. The rest is God's will.

These days, my motto is, "I'm doing my best and letting God do the rest."

More recently, I took a ride with Jim on our motorcycle. Earlier in my life, and even earlier in our marriage, that would have been impossible for me to contemplate, let alone do. The idea of not being in control of the motorcycle made such a ride out of the question.

Instead, I have found a sense of comfort, comparing Jim's driving of the motorcycle and my ability to let him do that to the way I see my relationship with God evolving. In other words, God is the driver, and all I need to do is trust him, hang on tight, and enjoy the ride.

Chapter Twenty-Seven

Thoughts

When you don't know what to do, say a prayer.

—Dr. Bernie Siegel

Recently I found myself thinking about my college years—particularly when I took a writer's workshop class that taught me how to teach elementary children to express themselves through writing. In order to teach that, you really need to try it yourself, and we did that—every day, for about an hour a day. That was dedicated, personal, completely quiet time where all I had were my thoughts and some paper and a pencil.

When I have time like that, precious quiet time, I can reflect and concentrate on what really matters. It is personal time for just myself and my relationship with God.

I can relax or at least attempt to, and that seems to be really important, especially on days when I have more physical pain.

It is amazing what you think about when you actually allow yourself an opportunity to do so. Normally my thoughts seem to race, and many times I have a hard time focusing long enough to accomplish anything constructive.

At work and at home, I find myself making lists just to stay focused.

Recently, I found my writer's workshop journal. Scanning my writings from that class, I came across one of my poems. Reading it reminded me of how much I could accomplish if I just dedicated quiet time to reflect.

<u>*Questions*</u>
In the faraway
Distance, I see;
Reflections of how
Things used to be.
Up high in the
Sky, so far;
Glimmers a dwindling,
Fragile star.
Its life was short,
Yet its reflection lasts;
Despite my knowledge,
That its time has passed.
How could something,
So bright, so strong;
No longer thrive
In the skies beyond?
A question seems
To persist in my mind;
Are we, in essence,
Really frozen in time?
Or are we like the
Fading star, now gone;
With someone watching
Us, from the great beyond?

Chapter Twenty-Eight

Just Another Day

The trees in the storm don't try to stand up straight and tall and erect.
They allow themselves to bend and be blown with the wind.
They understand the power of letting go. Those trees and those branches
that try too hard to stand up strong and straight are the ones that break.

—*Julia Butterfly Hill*

I was in seventh grade when my Grandma Connors died. I clearly remember my father describing to me years later the moment my grandfather said, upon learning of her death, "Isn't it something how one moment can change your life forever?"

Those moments can be both celebrations—like the birth of a child or the moment when you look into your partner's eyes and say "I do"—or they can be incredibly sad—like witnessing the death of a loved one.

I remember one life-changing moment I experienced that can't be compared to birth or death, yet seemed to weigh equally on me.

Each summer for seventeen years, I had returned to my job the week before school officially started. I would go through summer mail, begin processing new library materials, check purchase orders, the typical procedures you like to tackle before all of the other staff members return for the fall.

I chatted with the school secretary about how her summer went, asked a few favors of the school custodian, and caught up with a few classroom teachers who stopped by to visit.

This particular summer had been different from those before. Recent budget cuts and a worsening economy weighed heavily on my mind. Jim had been laid off a few months earlier, and the recession had become more than a topic of conversation—it was a personal reality.

I had experienced many changes in my life, but one thing had remained the same: my job. Don't get me wrong—the libraries I worked and taught in had evolved over the years, as had I.

When I began as a school librarian in 1992, we still used handwritten checkout cards and had one computer with Internet access in the library. Our computer lab consisted of Apple IIGS computers with the traditional "drill and kill" programs that left little room for creativity and innovation. I can remember weeding out old filmstrips from the 1930s and geography books copyrighted in the 1940s. Now I was processing our new audiobook collection made up of compact discs and Playaways.

Computer automation involved days of volunteers and my assistant working with me to match card-catalog records with barcodes. Thousands of books, magazines, and videos had to each be handled, matched, and processed—a procedure that is very time-consuming but necessary for automation to occur.

Libraries are like that; they don't run themselves. I often compare the operation of a library to that of a fine restaurant. When you go to a fine restaurant, you usually encounter excellent service, delicious food, and a relaxing atmosphere. If it is done well, you come away not only satisfied but eager to return. A good library is the same, except that the food is replaced with library materials and technology access.

Like a great restaurant, great libraries can only provide those services thanks to dedicated behind-the-scenes labor that the general public is usually unaware of.

A library is like a living organism—it needs nourishment, love, and attention in order to survive. I had been a witness to all of these changes and was very proud of that.

I enjoyed where I worked and the people I worked with. When you dedicate such a large portion of your life to your career, it becomes very personal to you. Over the years, literally thousands of students had walked through the doors of my libraries, and I had been teaching long enough to now be teaching former students' children.

I knew my libraries inside and out. If you asked me for a specific title, nine times out of ten I could walk over to the exact shelf and pull it off. I remember one year when a third-grade class was in the library, and I was helping students during checkout time. While one student was talking to me, another came up and asked for a specific book. It happened to be on the shelf I was leaning against. When I bent over and picked it off the shelf and handed it to the student, he smiled and said, "Boy, you are good!"

Back on that seemingly typical end-of-summer day, the phone rang and I answered it. It was my principal asking if I would be around for the next half hour. I replied that I would, and we planned to meet before lunch.

I went across the hallway and talked to the teacher next door. Time flew by, and before I knew it, it was time for our meeting—a meeting that would end one chapter of my life and begin another. A moment that would change my life forever.

Chapter Twenty-Nine

One Moment

Bravery is being the only one who knows you are afraid.

—Franklin P. Jones

I followed my principal and a well-dressed woman I had not met before into the library. We all sat down at a table, and my principal introduced me to her. She was the principal of the elementary school my friend Lois used to work at.

He then reached out his hand and gently touched my arm. His face was very pale, and having worked for him for a number of years, I knew that whatever he was about to tell me was difficult for him.

"Sheila—I don't know how to tell you this but …" he paused, "you don't work here anymore."

I felt like someone had just kicked me in the stomach.

"What do you mean?" I asked.

"You have been transferred to Riverside."

The conversation continued, and I hope whatever I said made a good impression. But looking back on it, I honestly don't remember. All I knew was school was starting next week, and I had three days to move myself out of where I had worked for the last sixteen years and into a newer, much larger library—the library that Lois had created and worked in for twenty-four years.

After the brief meeting ended, I walked over to the phone and called Jim. He was as shocked as I was, but he pointed out that I should view this as a promotion—after all, I had a lot of experience, and they must have felt that I could handle such a surprise move.

I called Linda next. She had been my library assistant for the past ten years and, because of these same budget cuts, had to leave her job with me for another in the district. She graciously volunteered to come over that afternoon and help me pack up.

My goal that afternoon was to pack up as much as we could as quickly as we could. I really didn't want to face any of my colleagues yet, because leaving so unexpectedly was all too fresh and too painful.

All I can say is, it is amazing what you accumulate over the years. The task was a large one, but looking back, I was very fortunate to have such thoughtful friends who gave their personal time to help me out.

Later that evening, I went over to my new school. As I walked around Lois's old library and now my new one, I couldn't help but wonder how this fit into God's plan. There have certainly been some twists and turns along my journey, and this was definitely another direction I was going in—one that had not been in my plans.

I pulled open a filing cabinet and randomly pulled out a file. Lois's handwriting was plain to see. Another friend of mine had worked in this library for the last four years, between Lois and myself, and her touches could seen in many places. But as I sat in Lois's old chair, I could feel her presence. She may have been gone for four years, but her memory was still fresh in my mind. You can't work anywhere for that many years and not leave a part of yourself behind.

I called one of my dear friends, Cheryl, over the weekend. She had been my friend for twenty years. She was one of my professors in college and had been an academic and public librarian for many years. She also knew me "several Sheilas" ago, watching me evolve as a person and a professional for a long time.

I asked her many professional questions, and she gave me a lot of good advice. But perhaps the best observation she made was on a much more personal level. When I told her how hard it would be for me to work where my dear friend used to, she immediately replied, "Well, maybe God wants you to spend more time with Lois. Look at it this way—now you get to spend time with her every day."

It was comforting thoughts like that one, and the patience of my many new colleagues and fellow librarians, that helped me during that school year.

Chapter Thirty

Tomorrow Is Another Day

*Be content with what you have, for God has said, "Never will
I leave you; never will I forsake you." So say with confidence,
"The Lord is my helper; I will not be afraid."*

—Hebrews 13:5,6

To say that chronic illness and depression don't usually go together would be, in my opinion, an incredible misstatement. It has been a dual battle for me for quite some time now.

I would like to explain, though, the misconception that I feel many make about depression. There are people who tend to believe that you are depressed, therefore you are sick. Actually, for me and I believe many others, the exact opposite is true—you get sick, therefore you get depressed.

It is a difficult challenge to face chronic pain on a daily basis, and there are times when you can get very down about the situation. It is hard to cover up that pain with constant smiles and an upbeat attitude. But it is something that I do really work at.

My demeanor is one that could best be described as serious-looking, and at its worst, it might be described as unfriendly. I am in a state of constant contemplation, over-thinking and analyzing every situation and every person I come across. I am naturally an introvert and have what some would call a poker face. I am a difficult person to read but not a difficult person to like or love.

I like to point out to those who make such observations that my calm demeanor is actually a positive quality.

Overly excited people make me nervous. Even as a child, I found myself gravitating toward people who were more calm and quiet.

As a teacher and librarian, my ability to appear to be the "calm within the storm" has gotten me through many challenging days and many equally challenging student behaviors. I have had former students over the years who complimented me on my ability to never lose control of my emotions. The few times I have, I have always regretted it.

But sometimes, I think that calmness comes with a price. My ability to absorb everything around me leaves me with no outlet. Sometimes I wonder if the autoimmune diseases I have are the result of not letting go of emotionally painful memories and experiences.

Depression is a very serious condition in and of itself. When I have down days, I turn to those who can cheer me up and give me support. For some of us, life has presented a little more to deal with than others. Fortunately for me, I have an outstanding supporting cast.

For those who don't know what it feels like, I would describe depression as a huge, dark hole. You feel that there is no hope whatsoever for your situation. You are at the bottom of this hole, and there is not even a glimmer of light to turn toward.

It is the most helpless and hopeless feeling imaginable. When you reach that point, you know you need someone, anyone to help you out. Someone to point out that little sliver of light that is shining, that is just within your reach if you are willing to try to lean toward it.

During one particular down day, I became angry with God. My life seemed like it was spinning out of control, and I found myself alone in that dark place. I remember sitting on the floor in our family room. It was nighttime, it was raining, I was in pain, and I had had enough.

I grabbed my Bible and cried out loud to God, "Give me a sign. Let me know that you hear me."

I flung open that Bible and placed my finger on the open page. It landed on Psalm 6—Prayer in Time of Distress.

> O Lord, reprove me not in your anger,
> nor chastise me in your wrath.
> Have pity on me, O Lord, for I am languishing;

Heal me, O Lord, for my body is in terror;
My soul, too, is utterly terrified;
But you, O Lord, how long …?

Return, O Lord, save my life;
Rescue me because of your kindness,
For among the dead no one remembers you;
In the nether world who gives you thanks?

I am wearied with sighing;
Every night I flood my bed with weeping;
I drench my couch with my tears.
My eyes are dimmed with sorrow;
They have aged because of all my foes.

Depart from me, all evildoers,
For the Lord has heard the sound of my weeping;
The Lord has heard my plea;
The Lord has accepted my prayer.
All my enemies shall be put to shame in utter terror;
They shall fall back in sudden shame.

Needless to say, I believe God is with us, always, even in the darkest of times. Face your fears and keep moving forward.

Tomorrow is another day.

Chapter Thirty-One

A Small Reminder

Every day is a new beginning. Treat it that way.
Stay away from what might have been, and look at what can be.

—*Marsha Petrie Sue*

It was school picture day. As I decided what I was going to wear, I looked at my necklaces and picked out a locket. Inside it were pictures of Jim and Michael. I searched through my box of pins looking for that special one. I thought it would be appropriate to wear for my first school picture at my new school.

The pin didn't stand out for its beauty or its value. It was a rather simple depiction of a white cat on a black background. Nonetheless, the pin had personal value that went beyond money or notoriety.

A little over two weeks after Lois passed away, I was bringing in the mail when I noticed an envelope with a small lump in it. I checked the return address and didn't recognize it.

When I opened it, I saw it contained a pin, and with it was a short note. It read:

Hi Sheila,

This is Annette. I have a gift for you from Lois. She picked this out for you and wrote your name on the envelope and told me to send this to you for Christmas. Lois is spending Christmas with Jesus this year. Merry Christmas from Lois.

God Bless You!!

Annette

Jim walked over to me and asked, "That's a pretty pin. Who is it from?"

"Lois," I said.

He stared at me in disbelief. I checked the corner of the envelope, and sure enough, there was my name printed in shaky handwriting.

Since that day, I have worn that pin on special occasions—my father's funeral, my birthday, and now today, school picture day.

School pictures were set up and taken in the library, which at my new school was just as Lois described it to me many times over the years, the center of the building. School libraries should be like that. They are where you go when you want to learn and grow intellectually. Especially in a school setting, that is how a library should operate.

As the weeks and months went by, I had become more at ease in my new surroundings. I could see why Lois liked working here so much. My circle of friends had expanded. I missed my old school, but at the same time, I felt blessed that my world had grown to include all of these new experiences and people.

My principal walked up to my desk and checked with me to see how I was doing. I appreciated her patience and personal interest in me.

"Don't forget to get your picture taken," she reminded me with a smile.

As I got in line with my new colleagues, I looked down and straightened my pin.

Albert Schweitzer once said, "In everyone's life, at some time, our inner fire goes out. It is then burst into flame by an encounter with another human being. We should all be thankful for those people who rekindle the inner spirit."

There are many who have rekindled my inner spirit and have touched my life. Sometimes it could be something as simple as a hug or a kind word. I have learned that looking at each day as a gift and an opportunity to fill your world with good works and blessings will not only make you feel better, but it will also make the world a better place. Now that's a win-win situation.

Chapter Thirty-Two

Acceptance

Turn your face to the sun and the shadows fall behind you.

—*Maori Proverb*

As I came to terms with the words *chronic illness*, I found myself going through a series of stages. At first I was overwhelmed. All of the information that I was inundated with, all of the tests, all of the symptoms, all of the uncertainty about my future—I needed to process it all and come to terms with it.

Once I started to process what was happening, I moved on to obsession. I thought about my circumstances nonstop, and I researched, sometimes six to eight hours a day on the Internet. I was a librarian, after all, and I knew a great deal about the researching process. I was convinced that there had to be answers out there somewhere, and if there were, I would find them.

This led to the next stage—desperation. As I progressed through the mountains of information (and misinformation), I was willing to try anything to relieve my situation. I tried hypnosis, herbal supplements, and drastic diets (one where I gave up all dairy, sugar, and red meats, which led to losing twenty pounds and clumps of hair). Many of the changes I tried only made my symptoms worse.

After all of the trial and error, I went through an anger stage. I was mad at the world, jealous of healthy people who didn't realize how lucky they were to be healthy. After all of the disappointing results, I decided to just give up.

I was outside one day watching Jim playing with Michael and realized that if I didn't try to do something, anything, to make myself happier and healthier, I would regret it. Was I the same person as I was before the illnesses? No, I wasn't, but I had to accept that. I think that was the most difficult stage of all.

A conversation with my doctor helped me focus on the priorities of my life. It was a simple exercise but very valuable nonetheless. He asked me to use words to describe myself.

"I am sick," I told him.

He sat there and stared at me. "What else?"

I thought for a moment and didn't know how to respond.

"Let me help you out a little. You are unhealthy—this is true. But you are also a mother, a wife, a daughter, a sister, a friend, a librarian. You are compassionate, talented, thoughtful … the list can go on and on." He smiled at me and continued. "Let's count how many words I used to describe you. Nine out of ten were positive. The only negative is a significant negative, but it is only one part of your life."

I would say that I am now in the stage of acceptance. I have mourned the loss of who I once was and how I once felt and have now moved on to the next part of the journey.

Acceptance is very different from giving up. I still do several things to keep myself in the best shape I can. I eat well, but I don't deny myself indulgences on occasion. I exercise, but I use common sense. Walking is the best exercise I have found for fibromyalgia because it keeps everything moving. If you sit too much, you get stiff quickly.

Yoga is a great therapy for me. It provides gentle stretching, which sore muscles and joints need, and I find that the mental aspect of it helps to slow down the mind and allow it to focus on positive thoughts. My personal favorites are a DVDs by Peggy Cappy and one DVD I have called *AM/PM Yoga for Beginners*.

As I gain strength, I challenge myself more, but the key is to not overdo it. I go to a chiropractor about once a month for adjustments and to a massage therapist once every two to three weeks. My massage therapist also does Reiki therapy, which can be helpful too.

I continue to read about new therapies and medications, but I limit myself as to how long I research. I use a kitchen timer to give myself a time limit; once it goes off, I turn off the computer and move on.

Having hope for the future is the key. Using quiet time each day to pray and meditate is so important for me. Keeping my life in balance and listening to my body and the clues it is giving me are also vital.

Holding my son in my arms reminds me of all that I have accomplished that I didn't think was possible.

Chapter Thirty-Three

Staying Strong

In the depth of winter I finally learned that there was in me an invincible summer.

—*Albert Camus*

Anyone who has experienced marriage and is honest about it will admit that as soon as the ceremony and celebrations are done, the real work begins. Marriage in even the best of circumstances still involves challenges. When one partner has health issues, especially chronic ones, there is an extra burden that must be faced.

Is there an answer I can give to the question, "How do you make it work?" Quite frankly, I don't have any answers, except that having incredible patience and love has helped us both.

In this book, I have focused on the support and love I've received from my husband through all of this. But to say that we haven't struggled or that all of our days are sunny and rosy would be untrue.

We have faced the darker days together, and through it all, sticking together has made us both stronger. Speaking on my husband's behalf, it is difficult to watch someone you love feel pain; he wants more than anything in the world to help me feel better and be healthier.

Going through the acceptance stage is vital for both the patient and the spouse. When you don't feel well, it does reflect on those you love and who love you. But both people need to agree that a new "normal" now exists, and they will work through whatever needs to be done as a united team—just as God intended.

I would encourage anyone who reads this and has marital problems to reach out for help. Many times it is only a phone call away. Taking that step, even though it is hard to do at the time, can save something that is much more precious than you realize.

We live in a society that seems to give up too easily. Sometimes our biggest challenges come before our biggest breakthroughs.

One of the best pieces of advice I have found on the topic of marriage is from Barbara DeAngelis: "You don't develop courage by being happy in your relationships every day. You develop it by surviving difficult times and challenging adversity."

Chapter Thirty-Four

Hope for the Future

Children will not remember you for the material things you provided but for the feeling that you cherished them.

—*Gail Grenier Sweet*

At a recent Bible study meeting, one of my friends shared how she had started writing down some of her values and thoughts as a way to communicate with her children both today and in the future. Hearing that reminded me of how comforting my own father's book of poetry is and how reading his words bring peace to me during good times and bad.

If I were to give our son Michael a "top twelve" list of what Jim and I believe are the most important life lessons, this would be it:

1) **Treat others as you would want to be treated.** When you follow the "golden rule," you can't go wrong.

2) **Don't let other people determine your values.** Look around at the situation you find yourself in, and look within yourself instead of following the crowd. If you are the only one you know who is willing to do what is right, then you need to be the one who will make a difference.

3) **Know when to keep quiet and when to say something.** This value is a challenging one. I have personally found that listening to others as they share their troubles or their joys is a wonderful gift. When someone wants your advice, they will ask.

4) **Once in a while, step "outside the box" and try something new.** When you find yourself relying on routines, life has become too

predictable. Meeting new people and stepping out of your comfort zone opens you up to new adventures and creates new challenges that will help you grow as an individual.

5) **Don't judge a book by its cover.** Even though our society tends to automatically set a value on individuals based on their appearance, their race, their religion, or their material possessions, you don't have to do that. Please remember that what truly matters is the content of a person's character. Avoid judging others. Remember, "Judgment is mine says the Lord." In the end, God is the only true judge of all of us.

6) **Allow yourself quiet time.** There are times in life that require stillness, and it is during such times that a person can really reflect on what makes a difference in his or her life. Find a special place that you can escape to. Turn off the computers and televisions. Many times when you "disconnect" from technology, you find yourself reconnecting to your inner self.

7) **Remember to be thankful for all that you have.** This includes being polite and always saying *thank you* when you receive something and *please* when you want something. Also, take time each day to thank God for all of your blessings. There will be times in your life when troubles may seem to overshadow all that is good. Don't forget that no matter how difficult the situation you face, you are never alone. God is always there.

8) **Each time someone criticizes you, make a positive affirmation about yourself instead.** Statistics show that 10 percent of people will never like you no matter what you do to try to please them. So don't worry about pleasing everyone. Your Grandpa Connors said it best when he told me years ago, "Be careful what you compromise on. The only things you find down the middle of the road are yellow lines and roadkill. Stick to your beliefs."

9) **Be balanced in all that you do.** Moderation is the key to life. Any time you find yourself dedicating too much time to one specific area, you are out of balance.

10) **Be honest but tactful.** Remember you can be honest with your feelings and still use kind words to express them.

11) **Be kind.** Whenever you come upon a situation where you have a question of what to do, just ask yourself, what would Jesus do? He would be kind, help those who need it, and love everyone unconditionally.

12) **Follow your dreams.** You know in your heart what your passions are and what gifts God gave you. So use those gifts to help make this world

a better place. Try to wake up each morning and seize the day. Life is so precious and so short. Make the most of it!

Chapter Thirty-Five

Leaning Into the Light

There are simply no answers to some of the great pressing questions. You continue to live them out, making your life a worthy expression of leaning into the light.

—Anonymous

If there is one thing I've learned so far, it is this: the only thing you can totally control in life is how you react to what happens to you. Attitude is really the key.

Today it is raining outside. Waking up, I find myself in a common situation—stiff and in pain. I am aching in many parts of my body. Despite that, I choose to do my morning yoga, followed by prayer and meditation. The tingling in my hands and the tops of my feet indicate I might be catching a cold, or maybe it's just stress. My immune system is slightly revved up. I choose to keep busy cleaning the house to get my mind off of it for a while.

Today is Michael's last day of preschool. He started there almost three years ago. He has been blessed with wonderful teachers who have the God-given patience only those who work with preschoolers can possess. I used to feel guilty over the fact that I relied so much on the services of his daycare. But I have since convinced myself that sometimes the best way to be a good parent is to have others help you out when you need it.

Michael is an energetic bundle of joy. His inquisitive nature keeps all the grown-ups around him on their toes. It is funny how life works. I heard a comedienne say once that we spend the first two years of our children's life trying to get them to walk and talk and the next sixteen years trying to get them to sit down and be quiet.

All joking aside, I have a hard time remembering what my life was like before he was here. Soon he will be in kindergarten, and the next phase of his life, and ours, will begin.

Today I called a few of my friends I haven't seen for a while. I will be going to a matinee this afternoon with one of my retired friends. Keeping in touch with those you care about takes real effort, but it is so worth it.

Today I am working on more schoolwork. My school will open in about a week, and there is so much I need to do to get ready for another year. This is my eighteenth year of being a school librarian. Time certainly flies by quickly.

Today Jim is working on the boat and spending time with his mother at her house. As parents age, sometimes you find yourself in an odd role reversal. You end up holding their hand to guide them across a street instead of the other way around. As we age, we find ourselves at a point in life where there are many more yesterdays than tomorrows. But if you are lucky, looking back will provide you with the strength to look forward.

Today I am taking time to be thankful for all that I have. Dr. Tal Ben Shahar, a freelance writer and motivational speaker, once said that we have treasures all around us and within us—we just need to appreciate them and value them every day. And if we savor and appreciate all the treasures, we will have even more. How true that is.

Today I sent e-mails to my brothers and sisters and their families. I am recalling a visit to my brother's house and the renewal of my spirit as I saw my son interact with the family I grew up with. Connections to your past are great reminders of who you once were and still are.

Today when we got home I opened up a gift from his preschool teacher. It was a framed picture that I had drawn of our family for a school project. There was a wonderful note from her about Michael. It melted my heart with joy.

Today, even though it is raining outside, I focus on the light in my mind's eye—the positive thoughts that keep me going. I accept my day with all its challenges and triumphs.

"This is the day the LORD has made; let us be glad and rejoice."

Chapter Thirty-Six

Helpful Resources

It is easy to sit up and take notice; what is difficult
is getting up and taking action.

—Al Batt

I have been fortunate to have an outstanding family doctor who has always gone out of her way to get me in to see specialists quickly. Most importantly, she takes the time to listen to me when I have concerns. I consider her to be both my doctor and my friend. That is definitely a blessing.

Through my research, I have discovered some very helpful books and CDs that have assisted me throughout the last several years. Some of them are books dealing with specific medical issues, while others might be memoirs or religious books that inspire me to keep moving forward. The following is a list of resources that I hope are as useful to others as they have been for me:

Always Looking Up: The Adventures of an Incurable Optimist by Michael J. Fox. His inspiring story makes me realize how important a positive attitude is when dealing with chronic illness.

AM/PM Yoga for Beginners by Rodney Yee and Patricia Walden. I use the AM portion of this DVD every morning to do yoga. It is a gentle beginning to my day. I would also recommend DVDs by Peggy Cappy.

Anatomy of an Illness as Perceived by the Patient by Norman Cousins. This was the first book by a patient that spoke to the importance of taking charge of our own health. His ability to tap into his own body's remarkable healing system through the power of positive thinking and humor made this a revolutionary book, and it still has a powerful message today.

Boundless Energy: The Complete Mind/Body Program for Overcoming Chronic Fatigue by Deepak Chopra, MD. I have read many books on the mind/body connection, and this one stands out for me because of the ayurvedic perspective. I have used many of the suggestions in the book and found them very helpful. I have read several of the author's books, but this one is my favorite.

Cure for the Common Life by Max Lucado. I have also read several of Lucado's books and found inspiration in many. This one stands out for me because it focuses on how people need to discover their "sweet spot" in life—the job or life-calling that God has created them for.

Fibromyalgia Help Book: Practical Guide to Living Better with Fibromyalgia by Jenny Fransen, RN, and I. Jon Russel, MD, PhD. I discovered this book while visiting the Mayo Clinic bookstore. It gave me several practical steps to take to help relieve the pain and make life more bearable. It was a good addition to the information I received while at the Fibromyalgia Clinic.

Glimpses of Heaven: True Stories of Hope and Peace at the End of Life's Journey by Trudy Harris, RN. For anyone who has watched a loved one die, this book is a wonderful compilation of true stories involving hospice situations. Both my mother and I were profoundly affected by the experiences that were described in this book.

Having a Mary Spirit: Allowing God to Change Us from the Inside Out by Joanna Weaver. This is a great soul-searching book that makes you think about how you can make positive changes in your personal journey with God.

It's Always Something by Gilda Radner. I love autobiographies, and this one is my favorite. It has both the humor of a great entertainer and the moving account of her battle with ovarian cancer.

The Last Lecture by Randy Pausch with Jeffrey Zastrow. If you have not watched Professor Pausch's last lecture on the Internet, I suggest you do it as soon as you can. His positive approach to living with terminal cancer will make you thankful for all that you have and, at the same time, inspire you to live every day to its fullest.

Living Well with Autoimmune Disease by Mary J. Shomon. This is a comprehensive reference tool that gives you details not found in other resources regarding specific autoimmune diseases.

The Love Revolution by Joyce Meyer. I am a regular viewer of this fantastic pastor's televised sermons and have read many of her books. This one in particular stands out for me because it emphasizes the importance of living your faith, not just proclaiming it.

No Greater Love by Mother Teresa. I love Mother Teresa's gentle spirit and dedication to the poor and helpless. No matter what your religious affiliation, you cannot read her words and not be moved.

Peace, Love and Healing: Bodymind Communication & the Path to Self-Healing by Bernie S. Siegel, MD. I have lent this book to friends and family over the years as they struggled with their health. His stories of cancer patients and their families are hopeful and filled with the compassion that this special doctor has. I have also purchased many of Dr. Siegel's CDs for meditation and guided imagery. They are fantastic.

Positive Thinking for a Time Like This by Norman Vincent Peale. I can't say enough about the power of Peale's words. I read him daily because he gives me a positive boost that is supported by biblical verse—a great combination.

Sound Body, Sound Mind: Music for Healing with Andrew Weil, MD. Dr. Weil has written many great books, including *8 Weeks to Optimum Health* and *Spontaneous Healing*. This CD has provided me with a good way to end the day, gently relaxing my mind as I attempt to sleep.

Some helpful websites for me have been:

- www.webmd.com

- www.mayoclinic.com

- www.myastheniagravis.org/

- www.fmaware.org/site/PageServer